KNOWLES

A SEPARATE
PEACE

NOTES

Revised by W. JOHN CAMPBELL, Ph.D.

Bound to stay open

Publisher's Note

Otabind (Ota-bind). This book has been bound using the patented Otabind process. You can open this book at any page, gently run your finger down the spine, and the pages will lie flat.

ABOUT COLES NOTES

COLES NOTES have been an indispensible aid to students on five continents since 1948.

COLES NOTES are available for a wide range of individual literary works. Clear, concise explanations and insights are provided along with interesting interpretations and evaluations.

Proper use of COLES NOTES will allow the student to pay greater attention to lectures and spend less time taking notes. This will result in a broader understanding of the work being studied and will free the student for increased participation in discussions.

COLES NOTES are an invaluable aid for review and exam preparation as well as an invitation to explore different interpretive paths.

COLES NOTES are written by experts in their fields. It should be noted that any literary judgement expressed herein is just that — the judgement of one school of thought. Interpretations that diverge from, or totally disagree with any criticism may be equally valid.

COLES NOTES are designed to supplement the text and are not intended as a substitute for reading the text itself. Use of the NOTES will serve not only to clarify the work being studied, but should enhance the reader's enjoyment of the topic.

ISBN 0-7740-3360-6

© COPYRIGHT 1990 AND PUBLISHED BY
COLES PUBLISHING COMPANY
TORONTO—CANADA
PRINTED IN CANADA

Manufactured by Webcom Limited
Cover finish: Webcom's Exclusive **Duracoat**

CONTENTS

CONTENTS

John Knowles: Life and Works

John Knowles, the third of four children, was born on September 16, 1926 in Fairmont, West Virginia. At age 15, during World War II, he entered the Phillips Exeter Academy in New Hampshire. Upon graduation in 1945, he immediately enlisted in the U. S. Army Air Force's Aviation Cadet Program and proceeded to become a pilot.

After being discharged eight months later, (the war ended in the summer of 1945) he attended Yale University and graduated with a B.A. in English in 1949. During this period, he was an assistant editor for a Yale magazine. He also showed interest in creative writing and submitted articles to undergraduate literary publications.

From 1950 to 1952, he worked as a reporter for the *Hartford Courant*. But he left that newspaper for the more adventurous field of free-lance writing, which occupied him from 1952 through 1956. He spent some of this time abroad, touring Italy and southern France. It was during his travels that he wrote his first novel, *Descent Into Proselito*, which his friend Thornton Wilder advised him not to publish.

In 1955, Knowles returned to the U.S.A. and shared an apartment with an actor in the Hell's Kitchen area of New York City. In order to pay the rent, he wrote drama reviews and published some short stories (including "Phineas" in 1956). Knowles began work on *A Separate Peace*, aided by Wilder's advice.

In late 1956, *Holiday* magazine published an article of his on the Phillips Exeter Academy. Knowles soon moved to Philadelphia to assume the position of associate editor with *Holiday*. While still working at this magazine, he published *A Separate Peace* in England (1959) and then in America (1960).

The novel was a success and Knowles resigned from the magazine. At age 35, he embarked on a two-year voyage through Europe and the Middle East, recording his thoughts in *Double Vision: American Thoughts Abroad* (1964). While overseas, he published a second novel, *Morning in Antibes* (1962) and established his reputation as a writer.

Upon his return from Europe, Knowles settled in New York City for the remainder of the 1960s, dashing off to Princeton and the University of North Carolina for brief periods as an artist-in-residence.

Subsequent novels and short stories were published, but none had the success of *A Separate Peace*. In 1970, the year of his father's death, Knowles moved to Long Island, where he has become a permanent resident.

A film version of *A Separate Peace* was produced in 1972. Then Knowles went on to write his seventh novel, *Peace Breaks Out*. However, his best work, in the opinion of the critics, remains *A Separate Peace*.

List of Works

Introduction to *A Separate Peace*

A Separate Peace is one of the brightest novels to emerge from mid-20th century America. Finely written, it combines all the intrigue of a mystery with the depth of a psychological drama, yet it reads easily. Often compared to Salinger's *Catcher in the Rye*, this novel is much less sophisticated in both tone and content, yet it offers many moments of analysis which can be related to the reader's own life and values, in a gratifying way.

On one level, *A Separate Peace* chronicles the friendship between two high school boys in their mid-teens. Gene, the "brain," and Finny, the superb athlete, are roommates and inseparable friends. Yet there is a rivalry between them, which turns ugly and leads to the crisis around which the story revolves.

Knowles achieves moments of brilliance in this work. It is filled with powerful metaphors and poetic images, and draws the reader in effortlessly. Knowles' talent for depicting character and fleshing out behavioral patterns is substantial, even though there are awkward moments, when we wonder why something has been said or done.

This was Knowles' first published novel and, as such, it is a remarkable achievement. Most first novels fail not because of the author's lack of talent, but because the art demands a great deal of experience and technical know-how. Talent, inspiration and energy do not always suffice. We should keep this in mind when we witness abrupt character shifts or lapses in the time sequences.

The narrator of the story is Gene Forrester, a complicated young man with a tragic event in his past. The crisis occurs when, after a series of events, Gene causes his friend Finny to fall from a tree. The result is physical disability for Finny, emotional trauma for Gene, and catharsis for the reader.

This novel is good, but it is not great. It fails often to rise above the level of sophomore psychology to the realm of the universal. This is particularly true in Chapter 10 — Gene's treatment of "Leper" Lepellier is at odds with his usual compassion and understanding of human emotions. He experiences fear, to be sure, in the presence of the "psycho" Leper, but his reactions are entirely out of line with what we might have expected of him.

This is also true of Brinker Hadley, the stalwart young class leader whose interests are vast and whose power seems unshakable. Because of an isolated incident, he abandons all his local and school positions, withdraws from major discussions about the war and sinks into an almost cowardly behavior concerning his future in the military. It is quite unexpected, given the context and stimulus, since there is no adequate justification or cause for the behavior. At times, Knowles fails to convince us of, or explain sufficiently, the motivation behind his character's actions.

This novel originated as a short story. Perhaps it should not have been expanded into a novel. The action sometimes gets bogged down with details that do not significantly advance our knowledge of the characters or situations. It has elements of a soap opera (though without the melodramatic exaggerations), in that we find ourselves being led through the trivial moments of the day. Of course, these moments *are* part of the prep school day, but for reasons of economy, the novel would be better off without them.

The reader of this novel will discover strengths and weaknesses in both form and content. But these are less important than the novel's genuine enthusiasm and emotion. It has a definite message for the reader and speaks directly to the heart, even if less eloquently than *Catcher in the Rye*. *A Separate Peace* is a fascinating document in adolescent discovery and offers much for psychologists, literary scholars and fiction lovers alike.

After reading *A Separate Peace*, try thinking what you might have done or thought in situations similar to those in which Finny and Gene find themselves. If there is a universal message, you will discover it within your own experience and will identify with it immediately. This will make your time with the novel much more valuable and will help you to understand the many layers of meaning for which it is justifiably praised.

Characters in the Novel

Mr. Carhart: The chaplain at Devon School.

Gene Forrester: The narrator; he is a student, in a New England prep school, who forms an intense friendship with his roommate.

Brinker Hadley: The class leader; a young politician-in-the-making; he revels in the pursuit of power and strives to control his surroundings.

Mr. Hadley: Brinker's father, who boasts pompously of his military days.

Leper Lepellier: One of the quieter students at the prep school (Devon School); he enjoys nature and the discovery of unusual phenomena; he goes crazy during army training.

Mrs. Lepellier: Leper's mother; a good cook and a sensitive woman.

Phineas (Finny): Gene's roommate; he is a talented athlete and enjoys energetic, enthusiastic contacts with those around him; he and Gene are the two major characters of the novel.

Mr. Prud'homme, Mr. Patch-Withers, Mr. Pike and Mr. Ludsbury: Masters (i.e. teachers) at the Devon School; all of them attempt to enforce the rules, but often are outsmarted and outclassed by their students.

Quackenbush: The manager of the rowing crew team who comes into conflict with Gene.

Dr. Stanpole: The physician who attends Finny when he suffers his fall from the tree and, later, his fall down the marble staircase.

Plot Summary

The novel is narrated by Gene Forrester, who returns after 15 years to his alma mater, Devon School. Devon is a boys' boarding school in New Hampshire attended only by sons of wealthy families. The main part of the story, told in flashback, is set in the middle years of World War II, as the U.S.A. was entering the conflict.

Gene begins by reminiscing about his former roommate, Phineas, known as Finny, who was extremely gifted in athletics. The two were competitive from the start, with Gene having the edge in academic subjects. During the summer of 1942, they were too young for pre-service training, so they passed their time in the relaxed atmosphere of Devon School.

One afternoon, the boys went down to the river and decided to try jumping from a tall tree on the bank, out into the water. It was a risky affair since, if the jumper didn't leap far enough, he would land in shallow water and probably break a leg. Usually only the older students participated in this dare, but Finny insisted on trying it.

This frightened Gene, but he followed through with it. They landed safely in deep water and, at Finny's suggestion, formed the Summer Suicide Society. The group put all new members through the test of jumping from the tree and, as part of the ritual, Gene and Finny always took the first jump. But Gene remained fearful each time, almost as if he had a premonition.

As time passed, Gene began to resent Finny. He believed that Finny wanted him to spend less and less time with his studies. Yet he felt compelled to follow his friend in the pursuit of manly boldness and fearless bravery. (All of this is set against the backdrop of an intensifying World War.)

One day, when jumping from the tree, Finny is the victim of an apparent accident. He falls and breaks his leg badly — so that he is not likely to be able to use it properly for the rest of his life. However, it is not an accident that causes this injury. Rather, it is Gene who causes Finny to fall, by jiggling the branch on which Finny is perched. Gene is motivated by resentment of Finny's attempts to make him fail in school.

Gene fears that Finny will report him, but Finny refuses to accuse his comrade of any wrongdoing. When the fall term begins, Gene finds things very different without his roommate.

Depressed and uneasy, he opts not to participate in sports activities. The war preparations have begun and several of the school's employees have left for the armed service. To fill their spots, many of the students perform routine tasks such as shoveling snow. Gene is not amused when one day he becomes the butt of a joke: one of his friends muses that Gene "fixed" his roommate Finny so that he could have the room to himself. When various classmates enlist in the war effort, Gene decides to go along with them. But before he can do so, he discovers that Finny is back at school. He immediately forgets about going to war.

Finny knows that he will never again be able to compete seriously in athletics, so he decides to coach Gene for the 1944 Olympics. Emotionally, the winter term is dark, and Finny refuses to acknowledge the existence of the war. He has known pain and feels more mature because of it. At the same time, Gene struggles with the idea that he is responsible for Finny's present condition. He feels intense guilt and is unable to escape it. The war draws closer as the two boys' lives unravel.

Sometime later, all of the students gather in an assembly hall to discuss the matter of Finny's broken leg. Gene becomes the target of their accusations and Finny, disgusted with his peers, leaves the room in an agitated state. Outside, he falls down the steps and breaks his injured leg again.

He is taken to the Infirmary. When Gene arrives to visit him, Finny is unreceptive and cold. He knows now that Gene caused his accident, and he resents the fact that he is no use to anyone during the war with his broken leg. When Gene returns the next day, he is met by the doctor who tells him that Finny has died. During a routine procedure for setting the broken bone, some bone marrow apparently escaped into Finny's blood stream and went straight to his heart. It killed him instantly.

Gene says, "I did not cry then or ever about Finny. I did not cry even when I stood watching him being lowered into his family's strait-laced burial ground outside of Boston. I could not escape a feeling that this was my own funeral, and you do not cry in that case."

This puts an end to Gene's personal war. He decides to enter the service, realizing that World War II means nothing to him.

Chapter by Chapter
Summaries and Commentaries

NOTE: All quotations are from *A Separate Peace*, John Knowles. Bantam edition, Bantam Books, Inc., published by arrangement with The Macmillan Company, 1982.

CHAPTER I

Summary

Gene Forrester, the narrator, was a student at the exclusive Devon School fifteen years before the novel begins. Returning to his alma mater, he finds it more sedate than he had remembered. When he was a student there, World War II was in progress. The school, since then, has had a coat of varnish painted all over it and Gene does not like its new appearance. The place looks like a museum.

Gene recalls having lived in fear during his time at Devon. Though he escaped this fear upon leaving the school, he relives it in his present visit to the campus. He wants especially to see the two places that hold particular memories for him. So after eating lunch at the Devon Inn, he walks back toward the school. It is a wet November day, right before the New Hampshire winter sets in.

Gene had undergone a deeply disturbing event while still a student at Devon. *A Separate Peace* is the story of this event, which Gene begins in this first chapter to examine.

Moving across the Far Commons, Gene reaches the First Academy Building, with its marble foyer and old staircase. He decides that the building has not changed much and proceeds to the Playing Fields. Devon is both scholarly and athletic, so the fields are vast and constantly in use. At the end of them lies a small river. And though he has to walk across wet, muddy fields in order to reach his destination, Gene plods on with determination. He has to see a certain tree — the tree where so many of his problems began.

He arrives at the site. As he stares at the tree, he thinks to himself that "nothing endures, not a tree, not love, not even a death by violence." The tree seems shriveled to him, smaller than he recalled it. But simply seeing it again is all he wants. He is now able to walk away from it and retrace his steps across the soggy field.

Then Gene thinks back to the time when he was a student. His roommate Phineas, called Finny, wanted him to climb that tree. Then, it seemed a large, dangerous tree that Gene refused to go near. But Finny, in his hypnotic voice, said that it would be a cinch to climb it.

Three other boys were with Gene and Finny as they looked at the massive tree, which had a large branch that extended toward the river:

> Standing on this limb, you could by a prodigious effort jump far enough out into the river for safety. So we had heard. At least the seventeen-year-old bunch could do it; but they had a crucial year's advantage over us. No Upper Middler, which was the name for our class in the Devon School, had ever tried. Naturally Finny was going to be the first to try, and just as naturally he was going to inveigle others, us, into trying it with him.

This took place during the Summer Session; they were not even Upper Middlers yet. The class above them was a class of seniors who were being prepared for the war. Jumping from this tree was part of their physical hardening program.

Finny was an extraordinary athlete, whereas Gene was an accomplished scholar-in-the-making. When Finny asked his friends who wanted to jump first, no one replied. So he stripped off his clothes, climbed the tree like a panther, announced that it was his contribution to the war effort, and jumped, plunging into the water.

When he surfaced, he claimed it was the most fun he had had all week. Gene's turn was next. He was terrified, but climbed the tree nonetheless. He discovered that the limb was thinner than it looked from the ground and that it did not extend out over the water. He would have to spring far out or risk falling into the shallow water next to the bank.

As Finny ordered him to jump, Gene wondered why he allowed himself to be conned into such stupid things by his roommate. But he hurled himself from the tree, landed safely, and enjoyed the rush of congratulations afterward. Elwin Lepellier, better known as "Leper", said Gene's jump was more impressive than Finny's. When Finny challenged Leper to jump, the youth froze. The other two boys, Chet Douglass and Bobby Zane, protested that school regulations forbade them to do this.

Finny concluded that only he and Gene had the courage to jump. The two walked back across the fields together, with Finny joking that he had shamed Gene into jumping. They horsed around, tripping each other and engaging in a wrestling match on the field. The dinner bell had rung and the other boys insisted they hurry so as not to be late. Finny and Gene decided to skip dinner.

They returned to their room and worked at their homework. After awhile, they got ready for bed and turned out the lights.

Commentary

A novel's first chapter always has the task of setting forth the necessary names, dates, times and places so that we can get involved in the story that is about to unravel. Such is the case with this chapter. The two principal characters, Finny and Gene, are introduced, along with a host of minor characters sketched in briefly for future reference. Finny is the athlete. Though he is not the most well-built athlete Gene has ever seen, he nonetheless carries himself with assurance and purpose. Gene, on the other hand, is more comfortable with his school work. His interest lies primarily in studying and getting good grades, but he finds himself drawn into the magnetizing orbit of his roommate, Finny.

Gene does not like to be swayed from his studies, but likes even less the idea of seeming a coward or fool in comparison with the dashing Finny. He is determined to keep up the facade of courage, even though he cringes at the thought of jumping from the tree. For Finny, there is an association, even if unconscious, between the war and the tree. Since the seniors use this tree to practise their physical training, it has become associated with the discipline of war and the need for strength. This intrigues Finny and he shouts in delight that this jump is his contribution to the war effort.

When we return to a place we knew in the past, it always seems different to us in some way. Gene finds this to be true of Devon. It is more sedate under the coat of varnish, but this impression no doubt has to do with the absence of familiar faces, the echo of a conflict which has long since been ended, and the idea that somewhere in the past a moment of horror has given way to the silence of death. Perhaps this is why Gene compares Devon to a museum, a place that we associate with inactivity, preserved objects and silence.

The narrative technique used here is the flashback. Whether *A Separate Peace* is autobiographical is beside the point. More significant is the drama that develops and the manner of resolution chosen by Gene Forrester, the narrator. He begins in the present, relating his recent visit to Devon after a fifteen-year absence. Within pages of the novel's opening, he shifts into the past, to the summer of 1942, when he and Finny were students at Devon. This flashback will prevail throughout the novel, as we learn the truth about what really happened in that summer session of 1942.

For Gene, Finny is something of a hero. He is strong, confident, physically well developed and persuasive in manner. The novel is set against the backdrop of World War II, and Gene sees Finny as someone who represents the values required in both a leader and a fighter.

The notion of war is important. It has at least three different aspects: (1) the literal aspect of World War II, (2) the personal "war" between Gene and Finny, which occurs exclusively in the mind of Gene (although Finny enjoys their competitiveness) and (3) the competition and rivalry that exists on the Devon campus, where athletics reign supreme. We have not yet seen what Finny and Gene think about World War II, but we can conclude that they are not too involved in it, emotionally.

Though Gene is terrified about jumping from the tree, the experience proves to be exhilarating. He discovers pleasure in the act of violating his former principles and sees the fun of breaking with tradition. The jump, then, represents something of a liberation from his strait-laced ideas and values. He returns to the dormitory with Finny and, on the way, senses a change within himself: "I abruptly resented the bell and my West Point stride and hurrying and conforming. Finny was right." From this point on, it will be a battle between Gene's basic philosophy of life and the alluring lifestyle represented by Finny.

CHAPTER 2

Summary

Mr. Prud'homme, the substitute Master at Devon for the summer, pays a visit to the two boys the next morning. Their absence from dinner has been noticed, and Finny explains that they were too preoccupied to attend. Finny doesn't mind being punished, if it is done in some novel and interesting way. So he explains that they had been jumping from the tree, even though he knows that this is even more forbidden than missing a meal. He reasons that the draft age may be lowered to 17 and that they may need to be ready at any time for the war's rigors.

Mr. Prud'homme lets Finny and Gene off the hook. At summer school, discipline is more lenient than it is during the regular school year. There is more tolerance. Finny decides that the teachers are "beginning to show commendable signs of maturity."

Gene attributes this lenient treatment to Finny's personality. The boy possesses both a "calm ignorance of the rules" and a "winning urge to be good." The faculty gives up on Finny, with the result that they weaken their rules for him as well as for the other students. This demonstrates the effect that Finny has on everyone.

But more significantly, the students remind their teachers of peace: the boys are not yet registered with a draft board and are not associated with the war.

Finny is the embodiment of this carefree peacetime. But this does not mean he cares nothing for the war. On the contrary, he sports a finely woven pink shirt that he calls his emblem. Gene protests that it makes him look effeminate, but Finny is not bothered. His mind is on more important things — that is, his self-image as a future participant in the war. He is wearing the shirt to celebrate the Western bombing of Central Europe. Since the boys have no flag, Finny decides to wear his pink shirt instead. It is an emblem that symbolizes support for the West.

Gene knows that no one else on campus could get away with such an outrageous shirt, and he envies Finny for being able to carry it off.

That afternoon, Mr. Patch-Withers (substitute Headmaster for the summer) hosts a tea for the Upper Middle class (i.e. Finny and Gene's class). It is a boring, artificial party at which the adults chatter nervously while the students remain unimpressed. Finny talks about the bombing, but since no one else has read the news story, he is the only one to make comments.

Bored, Finny decides to provoke a discussion. He suggests that all of Central Europe should be bombed, with the exception of women, children, old people, hospitals and churches. This sets things in motion, as both Mr. and Mrs. Patch-Withers get involved in the conversation. She believes that the works of art should also be spared in Central Europe, but her husband grumbles that the bombers can't pinpoint their targets that precisely, and that no permanent art exists there anyway. Finny enjoys the fruits of his labor and unbuttons his jacket as though he needs greater body freedom for the discussion.

At this point, Mrs. Patch-Withers glances at Finny's belt. In his haste that morning, Finny had used the Devon School tie as a belt — a crime which would not be tolerated by the masters. But Finny explains that the School is deeply involved in the war, by virtue of its being in the same world, and that the Devon tie should be symbolically part of the war effort. Without intending to make a pun, he insists that his Devon tie is being used to "tie everything together."

Mr. Patch-Withers protests, but without indignation in his voice. He seems both amused and perplexed, and Finny is let off the hook once again. Mr. Patch-Withers, usually so stern, laughs for the first time that summer.

When the tea is over, the boys leave happily. Finny insists they jump into the river to clear the party chat from their heads. On the way, Finny says it is hard to believe that Central Europe has been bombed, even though there are daily news reports and photos that confirm it. Devon School, in the summer of 1942, is a site of peace and tranquillity in relation to the rest of the world — and the boys take full advantage of this repose.

Finny wonders if Gene is still afraid of the tree, and this bothers Gene: he finds the question a little unnerving. It is true that Gene sees nothing enjoyable in the idea of a jump, but he volunteers nonetheless to jump first that afternoon. Finny announces that they will jump together in order to cement their friendship. They will form a "suicide society" in which membership depends on jumping from that tree.

Gene christens the idea with a formal title: the "Suicide Society of the Summer Session." Then Finny climbs the tree with Gene and the two of them stand high above the river. Gene is farther out on the branch than Finny and, turning to make a comment, he loses his balance. Finny reaches out and grabs him, thereby preventing a fall and Gene's fear disappears instantly, enabling him to make the jump into the river.

Later that evening, while Gene is on his way to the library, he realizes the full danger of his near-fall from the branch. If Finny hadn't come up behind him, he could have fallen on the bank and broken his back, or even been killed. Finny had practically saved his life.

Commentary

This chapter moves us one step closer to the crisis. Gene becomes indebted to Finny for saving his life and realizes the extent to which he depends on his roommate. His feelings for Finny have become more intense, mostly because he cannot help but admire and be fascinated by him. It is important to note that Gene is now in a position of gratitude toward Finny and that his later guilt will be closely related to this debt.

The chapter gives us details about customs and manners at Devon. We discover that there are rigid rules about attending dinner, class functions and so on. These rules are enforced, for the most part, by the School's masters, a group of men portrayed as being somewhat grumpy and stodgy. The two mentioned here are Mr. Prud'homme and Mr. Patch-Withers. Both find Finny irresistible and persuasive, and both excuse him for erring from the norm.

The incident of the tree-jumping takes on a new dimension with the creation of the Suicide Society of the Summer Session. It is as if the two boys know already, on a deeply unconscious level, that there is trouble on the horizon — that their jumping might be fatal. For Finny, it will end in death; and Gene will experience emotional trauma. Neither is spared the consequences of their risk.

Finny is Gene's savior when the latter nearly plunges to his death. Gene, as a result, must acknowledge a form of debt, even though he resents his roommate for being so hypnotic. Then, when the "accident" takes place later (Finny is shaken from the tree by Gene), the symbolism of this first near-fall becomes obvious: Gene changes places with Finny and acts out his jealousy by bringing pain to his friend.

It is Finny's character that draws all of this attention. Finny is elusive, mercurial and riveting. He has charm, dignity and eloquence to a degree that makes him different from all others. He can get away with rule infractions that would ordinarily cause punishment to his classmates, and he knows how to manipulate events so as to bring about the greatest possible advantage for himself. With the Devon tie, which Finny uses as a belt, there is no question that any other student would have been fined, expelled or at least called to account for misconduct. Finny escapes all this, creating in the process a lively discussion that ends by amusing the schoolmaster.

What is it about Finny that accomplishes this? It is his energy, his drive and his desire to be unique. He refuses to buckle under the demands of a system that he deems restrictive, and opts for a freedom that allows him to explore. His character is firmly elaborated in this chapter, and we can watch now as this character interacts with the forces around him.

Gene is a boy of emotional ups and downs. He wants very much to resemble his roommate, yet his fears hold him in place. His conscience tells him not to get involved in the jumps, but his need for recognition propels him to act. This conflict will prove to be significant. Gene will need some way of getting even with Finny and the tree will be his means of achieving this.

It is clear that Gene would like to see Finny punished for his misdeeds. When this punishment fails to materialize, Gene's anger grows sharper. He resents the apparent lack of justice and wonders why some people can do things that others cannot. He is not aware, at this point, that Finny will indeed pay for his daring behavior. Death's final slam will terminate Finny's wanderings and will bring focus to the issue of injustice. While Finny seems to play out his life on the level of the gods, Gene is left on a more human level and cannot compete. What he seeks is a fair balance between Finny and himself — a way in which the two can relate so that competition might seem more reasonable.

There is an allusion to the Garden of Eden in this chapter when Gene describes the tree as "forbidden." As with Adam and Eve, Finny and Gene have orders not to go near the tree. They know that jumping from it is illegal for everybody on campus except members of the senior class. Yet Finny urges Gene to jump, thereby violating the rules. The metaphor is clear: the tree will bring about their downfall, both literally and figuratively. Finny will, indirectly, die from the fall and Gene will suffer remorse. Finny is the tempter, yet Gene, too, is a devil. Each plays with the other's destiny and the results are traumatic for both.

The idea of the tree is complicated. It represents for Finny something larger than life — a symbol of danger and thrill and desire. He claims to be uninterested in the war, yet no one on campus has a greater commitment to war than he. The tree is the object from which the seniors jump in order to harden themselves for combat. Finny justifies his jumps in the same way. He wishes to be ready for war when his name is called, yet he puts on airs about caring nothing for the war. We will find out later that he cares very much and wishes to be involved. So this symbolic interaction with the tree comes as a prelude to later moments in the novel.

It is an awkward time for the adolescents. They are privileged in one sense by being students at an exclusive school. No doubt each comes from a prominent family able to afford the amenities of private education. But we must recall that the story takes place during a bitter world war and that the peace at Devon is only apparent. Adolescence is never calm. It is a time of tremendous adjustment and change, and children becoming adults discover that the responsibilities of the adult world are often less enticing than they once appeared.

For this reason, we should see the struggle between Gene and Finny as something of a personal war, set against the grander and more explosive backdrop of World War II. While Gene and Finny are close friends and roommates, they are also enemies — at least from Gene's point of view. The struggle to destroy Finny parallels the conflict taking place in Europe. It is ironic that Finny demonstrates such interest in the Central European bombing. He will soon be the victim of a different kind of "bombing" — but it will take place in the tree that he finds so enticing.

CHAPTER 3

Summary
Gene knows that Finny practically saved his life but Finny

was also responsible for his being up in the tree in the first place. Therefore, he almost cost him his life as well. This is how he explains that it is not necessary for him to feel deep gratitude toward his roommate.

Finny, not content with the name "Suicide Society of the Summer Session," has added the adjective "super" to it, thereby emphasizing his tendency to see things in a larger than life fashion. The Super Suicide Society is an enormous success from the start. One night, six other boys sign up as "trainees" for the club. Nightly meetings are held to initiate them, and each night the Charter Members (i.e. Finny and Gene) begin the meeting with a jump themselves. Gene hates this rule, but Finny insists. Of course Gene can refuse but he does not wish to lose face with Finny. Inspired by a spirit of anarchy, Finny forms his own set of rules and imposes them on everyone during the nightly meetings.

So Gene cooperates and never misses a meeting. He is not individualistic or independent enough to assert himself against Finny. "It would never have occurred to me to say, 'I don't feel like it tonight,' which was the plain truth every night." Gene has not yet learned to obey his inner impulses: "acting against every instinct of my nature, I went without a thought of protest."

The summer progresses in this manner, and Finny elaborates a set of strict patterns whereby his Society meets regularly. The boys skip classes and miss meals in order to be present at the tree jumpings. But Finny is not as carefree as his behavior might suggest. Rather, he leads a somewhat structured existence and values a code of conduct which approaches the Ten Commandments in discipline: "Never say you are five feet nine when you are five feet eight and a half."

For Finny, there is no such thing as losing at a game. When you play, you win, regardless of the points scored. Sport, for him, is beauty, and the notion of loss is ruinous to this beauty. He does not acknowledge the fact that when one side wins, the other loses.

The summer sports program disgusts Finny, particularly the badminton games. The seniors are engaged in a series of calisthenic exercises. Across the fields toward the river, there is a wooden tower about ten feet high where the calisthenics instructor stands during their sessions. Since it is empty now,

Finny and Gene move toward it. When they reach it, Finny sees that someone has left behind a large medicine ball. He prefers any kind of ball to a badminton bird.

Some other boys approach them and Finny suggests they get some exercise. Bobby Zane suggests that their game should have something to do with the war — perhaps they should call it "blitzkrieg ball." Finny changes it to "blitzball." The game begins simply enough, but before long turns into a warlike activity. Finny throws the ball at Gene and tells him to run toward the river. When Gene begins to do this, Finny chides him for not sharing it with the others. "Throw it to somebody else. Otherwise, naturally, . . . now that we've got you surrounded, one of us will knock you down."

Chet Douglass pounces on Gene and knocks him to the ground and Finny lectures him for illegal conduct: the boys must keep their arms crossed over their chests and must not tackle the ball carrier as if in a football game. Finny continues to invent rules as they play and determines that Gene should maintain possession of the ball since he was illegally knocked down. Gene is not pleased. When one person has the ball, everyone else is his enemy and pursues him.

When Gene throws the ball to Leper Lepellier, the latter refuses it. Finny stops the game and explains the new rule: "The receiver can *refuse* a pass if he happens to choose to. Since we're all enemies, we can and will turn on each other all the time. We call that the Lepellier Refusal." Finny returns the ball to Gene, who, of course, wants nothing to do with it. It seems as though Gene is the one who must always carry the ball and be pursued.

Blitzball is the surprise of the summer. Everybody plays it. It brings out the best in Finny, whose athletic skills are sharpened each time he carries the ball. "To escape the wolf pack which all the other players became he created reverses and deceptions and acts of sheer mass hypnotism which were so extraordinary that they surprised even him; after some of these plays I would notice him chuckling quietly to himself, in a kind of happy disbelief." Finny's energy is boundless and Gene claims to be happy about having such a roommate.

Gene returns from the flashback briefly to reflect that the war period was the most important historical moment of his life. "The war was and is reality for me. I still instinctively live and think in its atmosphere." He sees the then president, Franklin Delano Roosevelt, as still being the president. The same is true of the two great world leaders, Churchill and Stalin. But for Gene America is not, and never will be, the land of plenty.

Gene remains impressed by what Finny was able to do, athletically, during that summer of 1942. For example, he broke the school swimming record which had been set two years earlier. (But since there were no witnesses, other than Gene, the record could not be officially changed; and Finny refused to perform again for the coaches. He broke the record only because he knew he was capable of it. That was all that interested him. This shocked Gene, who wanted to see his friend duly honored for his achievement.)

Walking back to the dormitory after the swim, Finny suggests they go to the beach, which is hours away by bicycle. He believes that ocean swimming is the only real kind of swimming. It is not as "screwy" as swimming in a pool.

The beach, like the jumping tree, is forbidden to them, and Gene worries about studying for a test the next day and about being expelled. But he agrees to accompany Finny, against his better judgment. The tide is high and Gene is tossed about by a huge wave. Finny stays in the water for an hour, then they eat hot dogs, walk along the Boardwalk, and eventually buy beers (after lying about their ages).

Finally they find a spot among some sand dunes at the lonely end of the beach and settle down for the night. Finny expresses thanks to Gene for accompanying him to the beach. He reveals his innermost feelings about Gene: "I know I kind of dragged you away at the point of a gun, but after all you can't come to the shore with just anybody and you can't come by yourself, and at this teen-age period in life the proper person is your best pal . . . which is what you are."

Gene finds this comment courageous, and he almost replies that Finny, too, is his best friend. But he stops. "Exposing a sincere emotion nakedly like that at the Devon School was the next thing to suicide. . . . I started to; I nearly did. But something held me back. Perhaps I was stopped by that level of feeling, deeper than thought, which contains the truth."

Commentary

Finny is truly unique and Gene resents him for it. Insofar as Finny's athletic talents are concerned, Gene sees his friend as a powerful, accomplished performer. This is not what irks him. Rather, he is troubled by Finny's ability to sway him, to make him do whatever Finny wants. This hypnotic control takes away the independence Gene desires and makes him feel subservient to another human being. In the adolescent struggle for freedom and self-esteem, Gene finds himself living in the shadow of his roommate, and this bothers him.

To begin with, Gene hates to jump from the tree. He has never enjoyed this activity and is never likely to. So the creation of the Super Suicide Society comes as an additional tension since it means having to jump regularly, as part of the Charter Members' rules. "I never got inured to the jumping. At every meeting the limb seemed higher, thinner, the deeper water harder to reach. Every time, when I got myself into position to jump, I felt a flash of disbelief that I was doing anything so perilous. But I always jumped. Otherwise I would have lost face with Phineas, and that would have been unthinkable."

Why would he have lost face? Because during this period of his life, for a male, it is important to assert bravery and physical power before all else. Scholarship, which Gene has mastered well, comes second. Gene resents this. He knows the importance of a good education and feels threatened by the demands Finny's activities make on his time. Yet it is vitally important for him to keep up with his friend. There must be no question of inferiority or cowardice.

His cooperation, then, can be seen more as an eagerness to please, to go along with the crowd, to earn points in the mind of the all-powerful Phineas. The pursuit of scholastic achievement matters much less than the act of participating, physically. This is obvious in the blitzball games, where Gene seems always to be at the mercy of his many attackers. Like the real war, it is vicious. He is brutalized by his many "foes" and feels a need to strike back, to defend himself by destroying them in his turn. Finny will become the ultimate object of this venom, but this does not occur in Chapter 3.

Badminton disgusts Finny because it is a "sissy's game." It represents leisure and dalliance rather than strength and prowess. Finny prefers the more masculine sports of football, baseball and so on. They come closer in his mind to the rigors of war, to the physical contact of fighting and battle. The sport of blitzball is of significance because of its similarity to a war game. As Finny says, "There aren't any teams in blitzball . . . we're all enemies. Knock him down!" By this, he means to underline the importance of competition, drive and dedication to skill. He is manipulative, shrewd and completely unself-conscious.

Finny draws attention to himself for a variety of reasons. But Knowles points out often that his character has boundless energy — and it is this energy that attracts people to him. Anyone with great reserves of energy is more likely to be of interest to others than those who are listless, tired and dull.

An energetic, young, dynamic athlete compels by virtue of his presence. Gene does not possess this kind of energy, as we see when the two boys bicycle to the beach. Finny pedals along merrily, telling stories, singing songs and performing tricks and stunts. Gene, on the other hand, gasps for breath and churns his way up the hills. The contrast is clear. Knowles emphasizes the radical differences between the boys. Recognizing these differences can lead the reader to an understanding of what ultimately happens during the crisis of the novel.

There is a hollowness in Gene's admiration of Finny. We hear him utter words of praise, yet there is an edge, a biting regret that fills his thoughts. It is jealousy, resentment and even a measure of contempt. Finny "could also shine at many other things, with people for instance, the others in our dormitory, the faculty; in fact, if you stopped to think about it, Finny could shine with everyone, he attracted everyone he met. I was glad of that too. Naturally. He was my roommate and my best friend." But were they really best friends, despite such confessions? It is something they both claim, at various moments, yet this is hard to reconcile with the indications to the contrary. During the blitzball games, Finny is ruthless with Gene, insisting that he be the ball carrier more than the others. At the beach, Finny calls Gene his best pal. Gene, however, resents Finny for misleading and alluring him — but he continues to pay lip service to the idea of their deep friendship.

Perhaps it is best to regard these fluctuations as typical of adolescent emotion. The boys have an obvious attraction to one another, but their emotions are confused and they have yet to pin down what they really feel. It is no surprise that, at one moment, they are best friends and, at another, mortal enemies.

One thing, however, is quite clear: Gene knows that Finny

prevails upon him to carry out actions which he would ordinarily not do. In this chapter, Gene begins to place Finny in perspective, seeing him as the one responsible for his being in the tree in the first place. To be sure, Finny saved his life. But Finny ought not to have insisted they jump into the river. Self-analysis plays an important role as Gene attempts to understand the trauma of his past.

We have seen often enough that Finny is a paradoxical character. He argues one way, then proceeds in another. It is this peculiar shifting of positions that perplexes Gene, for example, when Finny claims that there are no losers in a game, yet plays at blitzball as if everyone's life depends on it. We shall see in the next chapter that Finny's character will provoke Gene even further, causing him to re-evaluate his own purpose in life and find out what role Finny plays in that purpose.

CHAPTER 4

Summary

When Gene awakens on the beach next morning, the skies are gray and dull. Finny is still asleep, in fact he looks dead. The ocean and the beach also look dead and gray.

But color finally pushes through as the beach sheds its deadness. "Finally it was totally white and stainless, as pure as the shores of Eden. Phineas, still asleep on his dune, made me think of Lazarus, brought back to life by the touch of God."

Gene is aware of time ticking steadily away. It is about six-thirty a.m. and he knows it will take at least three hours to ride back to Devon. He has an important trigonometry test at ten o'clock and cannot miss it.

When Finny wakes up, he insists on having a morning swim, despite Gene's protest that there isn't enough time. They get back to Devon just in time for Gene's test, which he fails. It is the first test Gene has ever failed. But Finny allows him little time to worry about it. There is an entire afternoon of blitzball, followed by an evening meeting of the Super Suicide Society.

When Gene tries to catch up on his trigonometry later that night, Finny scolds him for working too hard. He accuses Gene of wanting to be valedictorian and head of his class. These are cruel things for Finny to say, especially when we consider the numerous times Gene has followed Finny's orders, despite his inner revolt. Gene cooperates with Finny, but Finny finds it impossible to see Gene's viewpoint.

Finny's statements about the valedictory address raise a defensiveness in Gene. He protests that he has no such ambition, that he wouldn't waste his time that way. Gene does not admit his real feelings in this kind of conversation. Even if he has no desire to be valedictorian, he most certainly wants to succeed in his studies. Since this desire has little to do with hedonism, war or athletic indulgence, Finny sees no reason to get excited about it.

Gene resents Finny for criticizing his desire to excel. Finny, after all, has won athletic awards. Why shouldn't Gene do well in school? There is room for achievement in both areas. Gene realizes, after a moment, that by becoming the head of the class, he would be on a par with Finny. They would be equals, though in different areas, and this equality is likely the cause for Finny's jealousy. That explains his criticisms. Indeed, when Gene puts the question to Finny, the athlete responds, "I'd kill myself out of jealous envy." Finny does not want Gene to be the number one student in their class.

Gene's mind explodes with this realization. "Up like a detonation went the idea of any best friend, up went affection and partnership and sticking by someone and relying on someone absolutely in the jungle of a boys' school, up went the hope that there was anyone in this school — in this world — whom I could trust."

Gene is so miserable he is unable to concentrate on his homework. He tries to find something positive to think about, and eventually decides that he and Finny are already even: they are "even in enmity," in their quest for self-satisfaction and definition. Gene accepts for the first time the idea that he and Finny are enemies, competing for success in different arenas: "You did hate him for breaking that school swimming record, but so what? He hated you for getting an A in every course but one last term. You would have had an A in that one except for him. Except for him."

Then Gene realizes something even more important. Finny has deliberately attempted to ruin Gene's studies, which explains blitzball, the frequent meetings of the Super Suicide Society and all the other diversions that Finny creates. Gene decides that Finny wants to share everything with him, including his D's in school. That way, Finny would still come out ahead: he is the superior athlete.

Realizing all this, Gene feels better. He has finally put things in perspective, at least for the moment. "I sensed it like the sweat of relief when nausea passes away; I felt better." This forces Gene back into his studies. He determines to excel even more at his school work. He becomes not just good but exceptional.

Written tests are the downfall of Finny because, there, he is unable to talk his way around things. As a result, he receives grades that are barely acceptable. Gene notices that the more he works, the more Finny works also.

Gene derives immense pleasure from his growing assessment of the situation: he has become the best student in the school while Finny is the best athlete. But the deciding factor between the two is that Gene is also a very competent athlete. "When everything was thrown into the scales they would in the end tilt definitely toward me. The new attacks of studying were [Finny's] emergency measures to save himself."

August rolls around and examinations are at hand. Gene feels less prepared for them than he would like, mostly because he has continued to attend the nightly meetings of the Suicide Society. He has not wanted Finny to understand him as he understands Finny.

The evening before their French exam, Finny arrives to say that Leper Lepellier intends to make a jump that night. Gene thinks that Finny has "put him up to it," to sabotage Gene's success on the exam. Gene makes a sarcastic remark to the effect that he doesn't believe Leper will do it. Angered, he gets up from his books and follows Finny to the tree. But it bothers him that Finny has not pressed him to come. Finny, in fact, has urged him to remain in the room and continue studying. What disturbs Gene is the realization that Finny probably never saw him as a serious competitor, that he had never been jealous of Gene at all.

When they arrive at the tree, Finny has an idea: he and Gene should jump together. Gene goes along with the idea because he is numbed by his new realization about Finny's lack of competitiveness. Finny climbs up first, up to the limb high over the bank. He ventures a little way along it, holding onto a thin branch nearby for safety. Gene follows him, but when he takes a step forward, he jounces the limb and sends Finny crashing to the ground, where he lands ". . . with a sickening, unnatural thud."

Commentary

This is a chapter of crisis. From beginning to end, it chronicles a series of realizations and discoveries that advance the plot and further our understanding of the characters. Moreover, it sheds light on Gene's and Finny's personalities, showing them in new ways and unraveling for us the mystery of their thoughts. But there remains at the end a shroud of uncertainty as we see the two characters at odds with one another.

The chapter opens with the idea of death. The beach is a deadly dull gray and so is everything that surrounds it. Finny, who resembles a dead man during his sleep on the beach, is compared to Lazarus. This opening note suggests events to come. It presents a tableau of stillness and quiet that will eventually replace the steady flow of energy emanating from Finny. We must recall that while Finny expends much physical energy, Gene devotes vast quantities of *emotional* energy to his self-analysis and analysis of Finny. There is perhaps a kind of balance in this energy.

There is no question that Finny has influenced Gene in a negative fashion. He has persuaded the latter to spend time with him when he really should have been studying. As a result, Gene's studies are suffering and he actually fails an important test. It is just the opposite of the situation in *Death of a Salesman,* where Bernard tries to sway Biff into studying: Bernard knows, as does Gene, that the final examination is important in order to graduate. But, whereas Bernard devotes himself to his math studies, despite Biff's athletic preferences, Gene goes along with Finny and neglects his schoolwork. The result is failure.

This negative influence causes Gene to feel even more angry toward Finny. It is a vicious circle: Gene wants to retain Finny's respect, but resents being manipulated; he must, however, continue to follow his friend so as not to risk losing the "friendship."

Finny, on the other hand, is not anxious for equality. He enjoys his position as the superior one and realizes that this position is jeopardized only by Gene's potential for scholarly excellence. Finny has no control over Gene in the academic area, and this fact threatens him. It causes him to dominate Gene's time and entice him away from his studies. At least, this is what Gene thinks.

But Gene does not want to evolve a clear-cut code of values for himself — not yet. He fears that Finny will catch on to his secret and begin copying him, thereby ruining the possibility of victory over Finny. Yet it is hard to believe that Gene would renounce his French studies the evening before an exam, just in order to comply with the game and prevent Finny from discovering his strategy. If Finny has not studied hard for the French test, no amount of last-minute cramming will be likely to help him. In this light, Gene has little to worry about and might just as well remain in the room with his books.

Instead of staying behind to study, Gene follows Finny to the tree. It is as if he had some deep-seated purpose for doing so. Knowles has to find some way of creating a serious crisis or turning point between the two, and this is the occasion for it. Gene thinks at first that there is equal enmity between him and Finny. Yet as they walk to the tree it occurs to Gene that no such enmity exists, that it is merely a figment of his thoughts. This makes Gene quite furious, more with himself than with Finny — or rather, with the situation. He feels trapped by his own inadequacies and knows that Finny is irrelevant to his conclusions.

So the enmity is laid to rest for a while. It has been based on a war-like passion for victory, which is revealed by a vocabulary of war terms and expressions (such as ''The new *attacks* of studying . . .''). But now it swings in limbo, without the necessary focus to make it a reality. Gene is confused about everything and, preoccupied with his thoughts, he hasn't the energy to be fearful of jumping. It matters very little to him at this point that Finny is suggesting a dual jump. What concerns him more is the fundamental meaning of all that has led them to this point in their relationship.

At the end of the chapter, we are ready for the crisis. When Finny climbs the tree, we feel tension mount because we know that something peculiar is about to occur. Then, when Gene jounces the branch (accidentally or deliberately?), we experience the full impact of the situation. Finny falls to the ground. At the same time, the sense of competition and rivalry, and the fear of jumping, ''fall'' from Gene.

The chapter ends on a note of cold satisfaction. We feel tremendous empathy for the fallen Finny, yet we must also acknowledge a sense of kinship with the newly-asserted personality of Gene. Both boys have shown strengths and flaws and each has worked variably on our emotions. Finny's fall signals that he is no longer the perfect athlete, incapable of error and superior to all challenges. He is humanly vulnerable and subject to universal laws.

But the real problem arises when we examine Gene's behavior. Did he actively attempt to harm his friend, or was the jouncing an innocent move in order to steady himself? There is a certain ambiguity here and, despite the accusations that will follow, Gene's motives can be interpreted more than one way. He is somehow guiltless, yet he will be held responsible for the deed. His action was prompted by an instinctive, almost animal-like, need to avenge himself and bring justice to an unbalanced situation. Once his foe is down on the ground, he himself can plunge victoriously into the cleansing waters below.

CHAPTER 5

Summary

None of the students is permitted near the infirmary, but they learn that Finny's leg has been shattered. No one suspects that Gene is to blame for the fall. The masters are particularly upset that one of their young, healthy students should be deprived of his happiness by such an accident.

Gene spends time alone in his room, trying to empty his mind of every thought. One night he decides to dress in Finny's clothes. It excites in him a sense of distinction, but more importantly, it makes him feel like Finny. He examines himself in the mirror, standing there in Finny's shirt, and feels he will "never stumble through the confusions of [his] own character again."

In the morning, the illusion is gone and Gene realizes anew what he has done to Finny. When Dr. Stanpole calls to him that Finny is better and can have visitors, Gene is surprised to think that Finny might not be hostile toward him. But the doctor assures him that Finny has no reason to feel hostility. Obviously Finny has said nothing about Gene's part in the accident.

Finny will eventually be able to walk again, but will never be able to participate in sports. His leg has been very badly broken. Gene feels intense shock at this news and he begins to cry.

When Gene arrives at the infirmary, he feels queasy. He knows that Finny would never accuse him of anything behind his back, but would make his accusations face to face. Upon entering Finny's room, Gene feels close to blacking out. Finny's tan has faded and he seems physically smaller. But Finny makes light of the situation by claiming that Gene looks worse than he does. This pulls Gene back from his faint.

Gene asks Finny outright how he fell from the tree. The latter replies, "I just fell . . . something jiggled and I fell over. I remember I turned around and looked at you, it was like I had all the time in the world. I thought I could reach out and get hold of you." At these words, Gene responds violently that Finny had meant to pull him down too. But Finny adds that he had only wanted to steady himself. He had noticed an "awfully funny expression" on Gene's face up in the tree, when he turned around for help. But he recalls nothing other than that he must simply have lost his balance. Although he had a feeling that something funny was taking place up in that tree, he has now dismissed it from his mind. He apologizes to Gene for the feeling.

The idea that he has viewed Finny as a competitor makes Gene want to cry. As Gene prepares to tell Finny the truth, Dr. Stanpole enters and sends him away. The next day, Finny is not permitted to have visitors and is soon taken in an ambulance to his home outside Boston.

Gene goes south to his home for a month and spends the vacation in stupor. Summer Session has ended and he can hardly believe the outcome of events.

In late September 1942, Gene takes a train back to Boston and gets a taxi to Finny's house. Finny is pleased to see him and not at all surprised. The reality of Finny's weakened condition is reinforced by the white pillows propping him up. They remind Gene of a hospital. Finny looks like an invalid.

The conversation becomes casual and this puts Gene in an awkward position. He wants to confess his role in Finny's accident, yet feels ". . . like a wild man who had stumbled in from the jungle to tear the place apart." Finally he summons the courage to say it: "I was thinking about you and the accident because I caused it." Finny looks at him steadily as Gene admits to having deliberately jiggled the limb. Finny denies it immediately, but Gene insists that he is guilty. Then he realizes that this confession is causing Finny more pain and that "this could be an even deeper injury than what [he] had done before." At this point, Gene begins to wonder whether in fact Finny is right — that he, Gene, did not cause the accident at all. He sees that Finny is in no frame of mind for the truth. Besides, he will be returning to Devon by Thanksgiving and they can discuss it then.

Gene fabricates a story about being tired and confused from the long train ride. He needs to get to Devon since he is already a day late. With that, he says good-bye to Finny, vowing not to start living by the rules at school. But he realizes that this is "the biggest lie of all."

Commentary

A Separate Peace evolved from a short story, as mentioned earlier, and many critics claim it never should have. There are frequent moments of inadequate transition and character development, and this chapter offers several examples. After detailing for us the most minor events and episodes of the Summer Session, Knowles draws the session quickly to an end, sends his characters on a month-long vacation, and brings Gene back on a train in late September. All of this takes place within two paragraphs and comes as an unlikely sequence to the otherwise realistic style.

Moreover, the novelist falls into a redundance and repetitiveness that are uncharacteristic of the skilled writer. An example of this redundance: "The Summer Session *closed*, officially *came to an end*." An example of the repetition: "At the end of *September* I started back toward Devon on the jammed, erratic trains of *September* 1942."

This is a challenging chapter and it takes us in many directions. It begins on a note of nostalgia, as Gene tries to cope with his emotions toward the injured Finny. He is not able to visit him or obtain detailed descriptions of his health, and this serves to complicate his already confused state of mind. In a moment of fantasy, he longs for total identification with Finny and decides to don his friend's clothes. He dresses carefully in Finny's outfit: "I put on his cordovan shoes, his pants, and I looked for and finally found his pink shirt, neatly laundered in a drawer. Its high, somewhat stiff collar against my neck, the wide cuffs touching my wrists, the rich material against my skin excited a sense of strangeness and distinction."

This process of getting into Finny's clothing helps him switch identities completely. He feels instant relief from his trouble and sees himself as Finny in the mirror. It is a form of alter ego into which he passes: "I was Phineas, Phineas to the life. I even had his humorous expression in my face, his sharp, optimistic awareness. I had no idea why this gave me such intense relief, but it seemed, standing there in Finny's triumphant shirt, that I would never stumble through the confusions of my own character again."

Later we discover that the role reversal has been taken one step farther. When Gene goes to visit Finny at his home, Finny notices a difference in energy level in his friend: "My God, what energy. . . You sound like General MacArthur." It is significant that Finny compares him to a military figure; we can see that war is still very much on his mind.

Gene has absorbed some of Finny's energy, and Finny lies in his chair in a depleted state. It is as if Finny's energy has flowed from his body to Gene's, strengthening his friend while weakening himself. There has been a complete cycle: initially, it was Finny who saved Gene from falling from the tree; now it is Gene who has caused his friend to fall. They have exchanged positions, and not only on the energy level. They interplay with one another on almost every level, complementing each other and conflicting and being quite unable to survive without one another.

The animal in Gene springs to the fore as he swoops down upon Finny. In the tree, he satisfied his almost animal need for revenge by jiggling the limb. Now he preys upon Finny and injures him even more by bludgeoning him with the truth — which Finny is not prepared to accept. Later, Leper will refer to this same savageness in Gene. But it comes from a primitive, non-social level of his personality; Gene does not cultivate it consciously or with malice. It is a protective mechanism that has developed within him for survival, and this same process takes over during his visit to Finny's home. He provokes Finny by yelling, "Kill me! Now you know what it is! I did it . . . . Now you know yourself!"

At the chapter's end, Gene makes his exit by saying he

needs to get back immediately to Devon. His excuse about being a day late elicits from Finny the response that Gene should not begin the semester in a conventional way by conforming to the rules. Gene promises that he won't do this, but he knows he is lying. He needs Finny in order to maintain a non-conformist lifestyle. Without Finny, he will fall right back into an ordered, structured existence.

CHAPTER 6

Summary

The Devon campus is alive with students, many more than were present at Summer Session. Reminders of the war indicate that all is not well in the world: five of the younger teachers have gone off to war; Mr. Pike has arrived in his Naval ensign's uniform and so on. But continuity with the past provides a link with peace. The same hymns are sung, the same sermon preached and the same announcements made.

But Gene knows better. He knows that Devon's traditions slipped through the masters' hands during the Summer Session and that standards were let down. "Still it had come to an end, in the last long rays of daylight at the tree, when Phineas fell. It was forced on me as I sat chilled through the Chapel service, that this probably vindicated the rules of Devon after all, wintery Devon. If you broke the rules, then they broke you. That, I think, was the real point of the sermon on this first morning."

Gene occupies the same room that he and Finny shared in the summer. But across the hall, in the room that was Leper Lepellier's, Brinker Hadley has now established himself. Brinker is this year's "dominant student . . . the center of all the excitement and influences in the class." Gene is not ready to give up the summer and he longs to see Leper's snail collection instead of Brinker's many files. The "gypsy days" of the summer are gone, replaced by the order and industriousness of the fall semester.

Gene is late for his afternoon appointment. "I never used to be late. But today I was, later even than I had to be." On his way to Crew House, Gene has to pass by the river. He stops to think about Finny — though not about the tree and the fall. He remembers with delight how Finny used to balance himself on the prow of a canoe "like a river god" and stretch his body into the air until a veering of the canoe threw him headlong into the water.

The Crew House is located on the Naguamsett River, the dirty, saline stream that leads to the ocean. This is not the river in which they had played all summer; that was the Devon River, clean, pure and fresh. The Devon School lies astride these two rivers.

Quackenbush, the crew manager, spots Gene the moment he arrives. He is an unfriendly sort, with no sense of humor or cheer. He has matured physically before the rest of the boys and has a rough, deeply masculine air about him. He lectures Gene about being late, but Gene quickly assumes his duties as assistant senior crew manager. It is a thankless position — all work and no status. Finny would never have tolerated it.

Quackenbush becomes argumentative with Gene, accusing him of starting late in his career as a team manager. Gene knows from that moment on that they are going to be pitted against one another rather than being co-workers on an equal footing. He is certainly no substitute for Finny.

Gene tells Quackenbush, "You . . . don't know anything about who I am . . . or anything else." Quackenbush responds with "you maimed son-of-a-bitch" and, with that, Gene slaps his face. Being called a maimed person strikes Gene hard. It reminds him of his friend Finny, who is indeed maimed, and this cannot be tolerated. After a brief skirmish, Quackenbush orders Gene from the premises, telling him he is not wanted around there.

Gene's fight with Quackenbush has more to do with protecting Finny than with asserting his need for respect. He straggles back to the dormitory, wet and empty from the battle and wishes he had hit Quackenbush harder.

On the way to his room, Gene encounters Mr. Ludsbury, the man in charge of Gene's dormitory. He is an intolerant, authoritative sort, with a bass voice and a British accent. His Adam's apple seems to move a lot as he speaks. He asks Gene why he is wet and, when Gene answers that he slipped into the river, Ludsbury responds, "I think you have slipped in any number of ways since last year. I understand for example that there was gaming in my dormitory this summer while you were living there."

Ludsbury condemns Gene for having partaken in such schemes and for having mistreated Mr. Prud'homme. Then he adds that there is a long-distance phone call for Gene to which the boy should reply.

To his great surprise, the call is from Finny. Gene dials the number, hears Finny's voice and is greeted by "Happy first day of the new academic year!" Finny asks Gene to save the empty bed in their room for him. Finny rambles on about how Gene was so crazy when he came to visit; but when he discovers that Gene has not allowed anyone else to be placed in their dorm room, this reassures him that his friend isn't really crazy after all.

Finny asks for a rundown on the latest campus news, starting with sports. Gene replies that he is serving as assistant crew manager. This dumbfounds Finny, as one might expect, and he cries out, "You *are* crazy!" Finny can't imagine why Gene would want to manage anything. Managing has nothing to do with sports. Privately, Gene rationalizes this in the context of his having given up sports. "I wanted no more of sports . . . I didn't trust myself in them, and I didn't trust anyone else."

Finny is not satisfied with Gene's excuse that he has no time for sports. He says to Gene, "Listen, pal, if *I* can't play sports, *you're* going to play them for me." Gene feels an immediate sense of freedom. "I lost part of myself to him then, and a soaring sense of freedom revealed that this must have been my purpose from the first: to become a part of Phineas."

Commentary

This is a chapter of nostalgia and also the first extended passage where we see Gene alone, without Finny. Gene suffers from the dual burden of having to succeed in his senior year and having to confront the brutal results of Finny's accident. Devon seems empty and hollow without his friend. The energy is missing and Gene finds himself in a slump, unable to coast in his schoolwork or do well in sports. The consequence is disturbing: he gives up sports altogether and feels inadequate in the classroom.

The episode with Quackenbush is significant. It comes as the turning point in Gene's attitude toward sports. He knows that he is a competent athlete and that he must participate in some form of sports while at Devon. It is a requirement. But he finds himself resentful of the structure imposed by the crew team and arrives late for the first practice. It is Quackenbush who causes him to focus on his purpose in sports: he needs secretly to find meaning for his life and must replace the meaning that was lost when Finny departed from Devon.

When Quackenbush argues with Gene, we know that the situation is impossible. Quackenbush is no match for Gene's wit, nor is he an adequate substitute for Finny. He serves to underline the fundamental void that Gene feels at Devon, in the absence of deep friendship and commitment to an activity. The idea of being an assistant crew manager comes as a major blow to Gene's pride since he knows that the position carries no status, benefits, or advantages. But he wants, somewhere deep inside himself, to be a success in athletics. This is a sign of his ambition to integrate part of Finny's character into his own.

When, finally, Finny makes contact with Gene and insists that the latter compete athletically for the two of them, Gene discovers new meaning in life. The pain of his loss has been hard to bear and he has experienced strange feelings about what he has done to Finny. Quackenbush's attitude exacerbated this tension, causing him further alienation from the Devon experience. "It wasn't the words [Quackenbush] said which angered me. It was only that he was so ignorant, that he knew nothing of the gypsy summer, nothing of the loss I was fighting to endure, of skylarks and splashes and petal-bearing breezes, he had not seen Leper's snails or the Charter of the Super Suicide Society; he shared nothing, knew nothing, felt nothing as Phineas had done."

Clearly Finny had become the single most important force in Gene's life. With this force gone, Gene was in limbo, in profound sadness and confusion. When he finds out that Finny is indeed returning to the school, he feels a renewal of energy and life inside of him — a resurgence of activity and desire for fulfillment.

Finny arrives in time to save Gene from despair, pulling him back from depression and withdrawal. If Gene has had a nasty experience with Quackenbush, so what? None of this concerns Finny. Finny will lead his former roommate back to health and glory, fusing their lives with radiance and joy. Their union gives both of them life. Gene realizes that this has been his purpose and he looks forward to seeing Finny again.

CHAPTER 7

Summary

Gene takes a shower in order to cleanse himself of the dirty water of the Naguamsett River. Then Brinker Hadley wanders into his room, looking very much the prep school conservative who is interested in politics, arrangements and offices. He is surprised that Gene has a room all to himself and remarks on Gene's "influence." Gene likes Brinker, but finds it odd to be thus congratulated by the class leader.

Brinker suggests then that Gene knew all along that Finny would not be returning to Devon — that he chose him as roommate so as to have the room to himself. This irks Gene, who protests that he had no such knowledge.

They decide to have a smoke and proceed to the Butt Room, a dungeon-like space in the basement of the dormitory. There are already about ten smokers there. Brinker seizes Gene by the neck and shoves him into the room. Someone asks what the charge is, and Brinker replies, "Doing away with his roommate so he could have a whole room to himself. Rankest treachery . . . Practically fratricide."

The room becomes very quiet and Gene takes violent offense to such treatment. A boy uncoils tensely from the couch and suggests that Gene killed Finny. Brinker jumps in to qualify the statement, claiming that Finny hangs between life and death "in the arms of his grief-stricken old mother." Gene feels it important to make light of the situation, so he announces that his only sin is to have dropped a little arsenic in Finny's coffee. This outrages Brinker, who is out to get Gene.

The accusations continue. Gene opts for a fictitious explanation to describe what happened. "First I stole all his money. Then I found that he cheated on his entrance tests to Devon and I blackmailed his parents about that, then I made love to his sister in Mr. Ludsbury's study, then I . . ."

Some grins break out among the students present. But Gene finds it impossible to utter the words, "then I pushed him out of the tree." He invites the executioners to complete the story, Sherlock Holmes style. When the younger boy, who accused him of killing Finny, calls out that Gene probably pushed his friend from the tree, Gene announces that he is quite wrong.

This demolishes the boy's momentary superiority and causes him to hate Gene.

With that, Gene jumps up and insists on going to study his French. He leaves the room and goes upstairs.

Meanwhile, World War II is still going strong. Many of the local harvesters are off in the army or at work in the war factories. As a result, the students have to help with the apple crop. Before long, an early snowfall shuts down the railroad yards. Students volunteer to dig them out, but not Leper Lepellier. He refuses to acknowledge that anything has changed or that the war is taking its toll on civilization. Instead of helping out with the snow-shoveling, Leper stays at the school to sketch birds and to ski.

On the way to the train station, Gene meets Leper on his skis, searching for a beaver dam. He is interested to see how the beavers adapt to the winter.

Gene spends the day toiling in the railroad yard, helping to dig it out. It is hard work — not at all the fun they had enjoyed in the apple orchards.

The students are able to clear off one of the tracks and watch the first train trundle into the station. It is a troop train filled with young recruits who are about the same age as the students.

On the way back to the School, the boys talk about the war, aviation training programs and brothers in the service. They think it is absurd to be studying dead languages when a war is taking place. In general, they find the idea of Devon School a bit futile.

Quackenbush announces that he intends to remain at Devon for the entire year, regardless of who else chooses to enter the war. He believes in the value of a high school certificate and does not wish to enter the army before his time.

Arriving back at the campus, they come upon Leper Lepellier, who is still on skis. He has found his beaver dam and is radiant about it. Brinker Hadley feels this attention to nature is outrageous at a time when the country is at war. So he shouts out that he is going to enlist the following day. Gene is delighted to hear it.

In fact, it intrigues him to the point where he gives serious consideration to enlisting himself. "To slam the door impulsively on the past, to shed everything down to my last bit of clothing, to break the pattern of my life." He knows that going to war will be "deadly," but knows also that everything he has ever wanted in life has contained "something deadly." If this deadliness was absent, as with Phineas, he put it there himself.

Alone under the stars, Gene grapples with the idea of enlistment. He decides that he owes nothing to anyone, but that he owes it to himself to meet this crisis in his life. He concludes that now is the time to enter the war.

He runs up quickly to the dormitory and discovers, upon reaching his room, a stream of light filtering underneath his door. He grabs the knob and swings open the door. Phineas is back. Everything that has happened during the day fades from Gene's mind as he finds himself reunited with his friend.

Commentary

War is the subject of this chapter: war abroad, war at home and war in the mind of Gene. The war abroad remains distant and irrelevant to the students at Devon until they begin to feel its effects. When school begins in September, they find that several of the faculty members have left to join the army. Large numbers of local people have also departed, leaving the students with the job of helping out with the apple picking. When the giant snowfall arrives, there are pleas for volunteers to clear the snow.

In short, the war is affecting even Devon School, despite its privileged location and elite status. Gene tries to look at it objectively, realizing that he must play some role in it eventually and preferring to make that decision on his own, before being drafted. In the first part of the chapter, when Brinker leads Gene down to the Butt Room for the confrontation with the other students, we see the symbolic side-taking that occurs in any war situation. It is Gene against the others and he must negotiate his way out of the corner in order to survive their attacks.

This enactment of a war situation intensifies to the conflict already taking place in Gene's mind. It is as if his greatest ally, Finny, has been killed in a battle, leaving Gene lonely, alienated and disturbed. The sudden emptiness at Devon alarms him, leaving him without direction or purpose. His grades have suffered and he has no interest in athletics. The athletic Finny and brainy Gene of the Summer Session have ceased to exist as such.

Finny survives as a shadow of his former self and Gene lives on as a confused and lonely child.

The issue of war arises in the contrasting episodes of the apple-picking and the snow-shoveling. When the students pick apples, the weather is still spectacular. The leaves are in full color, the autumn air retains its summer warmth, with only a hint of the cold winter ahead, and the boys enjoy the community activity involved in the task. The snow-shoveling, on the other hand, becomes drudgery. The weather is cold, wet and gray. They do not enjoy their co-workers, nor do they derive pleasure from the isolation and monotony of the task. When the troop train arrives, it reinforces the presence of war, even if the young recruits seem fresh and alive ("They seemed to be having a wonderful time, their uniforms looked new and good; they were clean and energetic; they were going places"). The young soldiers may look clean on this dull, snowy day, but their futures are uncertain and they are headed for dismal, dreary times. The episode underscores the notion that the Devon students too are clean, fresh and "going places." But they too will soon be caught up in the war effort and are already being indoctrinated, without necessarily knowing it, into the process.

The apple crop reminds us of the Eden motif that recurs throughout the novel. The tree from which Finny and Gene jump all summer is reminiscent, in one sense, of the apple tree that ruined Adam and Eve (it was the instrument of their undoing and caused their expulsion from Eden). Likewise, the young Devon students are soon to be expelled from the joys of the apple orchard and driven to the hardship of the railroad yard. The dirt, grime and hazards of war are already implicit in the snowed-in train station.

Gene decides in the end to enlist in the army. But when he sees that Finny has returned, his ideas and plans evaporate. The commitment to violence is quickly weakened when he finds himself face to face with his alter ego. In Finny he must find meaning, and in meaning he must find truth. The notion of doing battle is once again internalized: Gene does not go off to join the soldiers at the front. Instead, the battleground on which he fights is an inner one, in his mind. And the war he fights is more private, personal.

CHAPTER 8

Summary

Finny's first words are that he should never have left Gene alone. He is appalled by Gene's outfit (but Gene has just returned from shoveling snow).

Finny grumbles about the absence of maids. Gene explains that the war has made certain things impossible and that to go without maid service is not too much of a sacrifice for them, given that other people are suffering under far worse conditions. Gene resents Finny's moodiness over this lost luxury. In this way they have grown apart.

When they wake up the next morning, Finny complains again about the lack of maids. Then he asks Gene to hand him his crutches. This depresses Gene.

"Until now, in spite of everything, I had welcomed each new day as though it were a new life, where all past failures and problems were erased, and all future possibilities and joys open and available, to be achieved probably before night fell again. Now, in this winter of snow and crutches with Phineas, I began to know that each morning reasserted the problems of the night before, that sleep suspended all but changed nothing."

Brinker Hadley bursts into the room to discuss enlistment and is stunned to see Finny. It ruffles Finny to think that Gene has thought of enlisting. At this point, Gene realizes with a shock that Finny needs him, or depends upon him in some way. When Gene says that he is not going to enlist after all, Finny is tremendously relieved.

Finny suggests that since it is his first day back, they should skip their classes, and pretend that he fainted from exertion on the way from the chapel. He wants to see the gym, which is located at the other end of a large field of ice. They go there without speaking, and by the time they arrive Finny's face is covered with sweat. No doubt he has deceived his doctor into thinking that he is well enough to return to Devon. The truth is, his entire body is shaking from the exertion.

They proceed to the locker room downstairs, which leads to the pool. Finny looks around and examines the place, concluding finally that nothing has changed. Gene quietly disagrees with him, and this prompts Finny to say, "You're going to be the big star now." He can't understand why Gene has given up sports, and when Gene replies that sports seemed unimportant with the war on, Finny asks him, "Have you swallowed all that war stuff?" It is as if Finny has no feelings about, or belief in, the reality of the war.

For him, the war is merely a story invented by "fat old men" to keep younger people from crowding them out of their jobs. This same group of men invented the Depression and Prohibition, to further their own lot at the expense of the millions who believe them. When Gene asks why Finny alone knows about these old men, Finny replies, "Because I've suffered." This creates a painful moment between the two and Gene instinctively begins doing chinups as a "grotesque offering to Phineas." Finny orders him to do 30 of them.

Finny explains, after Gene has completed the chinups, that his lifelong goal has been to enter the Olympics. He is not sure now that he will be able to train for the 1944 games, so he decides to coach Gene for them instead.

The two begin training on a regular basis. They get up at six a.m. and Gene runs before breakfast. With Finny's coaching, he begins to improve. Later in the day, Gene tutors Finny in his studies and Finny likewise improves. This arrangement is mutually beneficial and their relationship enjoys a new period of growth. In fact, Gene begins to believe that it is utterly impossible that there is a war.

Commentary

During their separation, Finny and Gene have grown apart. Much of the growth has occurred in Gene, so that when Finny comes back to Devon, there is a noticeable difference in attitudes. A case in point is the matter of the dormitory maids. Gene has had steady contact with the effects of war on Devon, whereas Finny has enjoyed the protective atmosphere of his home. The maids symbolize a bygone era when luxury and service were taken for granted. This is no longer the case, with the hardships imposed by war and the sacrifices — even if small — made by the students. It is not likely that Finny really cares much about the maids. This is simply an occasion for Knowles to demonstrate the drifting apart that has taken place.

Another change is evident in Gene's attitude toward the war, for he has decided to enlist in the army. This change is aborted when the two boys reunite. Gene forgoes his army decision and opts for a renewed existence with Finny.

Finny, on the other hand, has changed in a physical sense. He has been forced into a new outlook on life because of his physical limitations. As an immensely physical person, he finds it impossible to shut out his past. Therefore, he entices Gene into a devotion to sports, even though this is neither Gene's strong point nor his major interest. It is an example of Finny's persuasiveness and influence over his friend. Gene ends up adopting a lifestyle utterly unlike the one which he had begun to choose.

This raises an important point. Gene, during the Summer Session, was a shadow of Finny. He admired and envied him, while also resenting bitterly the fact that Finny seemed to lure him astray. During Finny's recuperation at home, Gene discovered what it was like to live without Finny. He was beginning to assert himself as never before (e.g. with Quackenbush). Now that Finny is back, Gene reverts to his former subservience to his idol, his alter ego. Instead of signing up with the army, he signs up with Finny.

For example, when Finny suggests that they skip class and go to the gymnasium, common sense dictates that they are making a mistake. Skipping classes on the first day of the semester; is the start of a bad habit, but what's more, it is dangerous for Finny to try crossing a field of ice while still on crutches. Yet Gene complies. Whereas he had stood up to the persecutors in the Butt Room as well as to Quackenbush, Gene now contents himself with a more passive attitude of acceptance. Finny's word becomes law, as though Finny is the only authority figure to whom Gene will listen.

This sets in motion a process of role reversal. Finny becomes the spectator and Gene becomes the athlete. It is an exchange of traits that ties the two boys even closer. Gene becomes active; Finny becomes passive. But in a sense, Gene remains passive in his devotion to Finny and Finny stays active in his determination to coach Gene. It is a truly complicated relationship, in which they relate to each other from deep internal needs: needs for love, fulfillment, strength and individuality.

Gene finds it difficult at first to believe Finny's theory

about the war — namely, that there really isn't a war going on and that the whole thing is a fiction invented by fat old men in Washington. But Finny's yarn begins to make sense to Gene: it is not out of the question for politicians in Washington to fabricate something that will work to their advantage. While the rest of the nation is eating porridge, the "fat cats" eat steak at their private clubs.

We will learn shortly that Finny believes deeply in the war and wishes, at all costs, to become involved. But his physical condition is such that no one will take him. For this reason, he is denying the war experience and pretending it doesn't exist. It is a form of self-defense, for Finny realizes that his greatest wish, next to entering the Olympics, cannot come true.

At this point, many readers notice a slackening of the pace and wonder if the novel ought not to have been left as a short story. It is tiresome to zigzag back and forth from activity to passivity, in the case of Gene, and to see Finny constantly rebuffed as an unfulfilled victim. Gene is something of a dolt in his predictable submission to Finny's wishes. But this is the situation created by Knowles to lead us finally to his explosive ending.

CHAPTER 9

Summary

Gene realizes that he has fallen back under the spell of his roommate. "This was my first but not my last lapse into Finny's vision of peace." Finny's theory about the inexistence of war entrances Gene for varying reasons, even though he has never really believed it. Now that Finny has returned, Gene finds life more meaningful and feels less confusion in his daily existence. Owing to this renewed peace, the war exerts little influence on him anymore.

The enlistment of Leper makes the war appear all the more unreal. Leper's act seems just another example of his unusual behavior. Everyone knows that he once slept on top of Mount Katahdin in Maine "where each morning the sun first strikes United States territory." So his decision to enlist surprises no one; he always liked to find new things to do.

In early January, a recruiter from the U.S. ski troops shows the senior class a film about the war. It is one of those highly idealistic, optimistic productions designed to entice young people to enlist. Finny doesn't believe a word of it. But Leper does. He believes in the value of the ski troops and, a week later, has left Devon. He is Devon's first recruit, though many others such as Brinker have talked about enlisting. The students are not very impressed by Leper's deed and rarely discuss him. But one day Brinker reads in the paper about an attempt on Hitler's life. Brinker remarks, "That was Leper, of course."

Finny disapproves of the comments that everyone begins making about Leper. He thinks Leper is completely incompetent and not worthy of mention. Gene remarks: "He drew me increasingly away from the Butt Room crowd, away from Brinker and Chet and all other friends, into a world inhabited by just himself and me."

As the winter drags on, most of the students become depressed about the dirty snow and dreary wetness of the campus. But not Finny. For him, there is neither war nor bad weather. He announces that it is time to organize a Winter Carnival. Gene heads up the snow statues committee and Brinker takes charge of the food and music.

Ever since Gene decided not to enlist, Brinker has become disillusioned with life. It isn't that Brinker resents Gene, but he needs company and moral support to do anything. He gives up all his campus and local activities, but agrees to work on the Carnival since it is Finny's first sign of renewed commitment to Devon.

Carnival Day, a Saturday, turns out to be dark and gray. Everyone cooperates with Finny's wishes: a prize table has been set up (with an odd array of prizes, including a lock of the town belle's hair); the apple cider is being carefully chilled in the snow, and a few pathetic statues are sculpted from the wet snow.

Brinker, who is standing guard over the apple cider, is impatient to begin the games. The other boys are closing in around him, and, at a word from Finny, they all attack Brinker and rob him of his apple cider. A fracas develops but is soon squelched when Finny demands that the games be initiated with a burning torch, as in the Olympics. So they douse a copy of the *Iliad* with cider and set it aflame.

The cider combines with the boys' enthusiasm to heighten

the merry-making. Finny gets up on the prize table and begins dancing on one leg, while Gene zooms into the air from the ski jump. Finally Finny calls them to order to announce that Gene is their "Olympic candidate." Gene feels very special. At this point, he would do anything Finny asked of him. This Carnival Day has proved to be an immensely joyous occasion for Gene, as well as for the others. "It wasn't the cider which made me surpass myself, it was this liberation we had torn from the gray encroachments of 1943, the escape we had concocted, this afternoon of momentary, illusory, special and separate peace."

Then a telegram arrives for Gene. Finny says it must be from the Olympic Committee, announcing that they want Gene Forrester for their team. But when he reads it, his face registers shock. It is from Leper Lepellier, pleading for help. The message states, "I have escaped and need help. . . . My safety depends on you coming at once."

Commentary

This chapter takes us to the high point of the novel, after which everything will progress rapidly downhill. Until now, Gene has experienced true happiness amidst his friends, especially alongside Finny. Now he must confront the reality of another human being in need — namely, Leper Lepellier. The suspense comes from our not knowing yet what has happened to Leper. But one thing is certain: Gene's mind is wrenched away from Finny and is directed toward someone who may be very much in danger.

References to Leper appear throughout this chapter. It is, in a sense, Leper's chapter. His decision to join the ski troops reflects a commitment of sorts to the war, yet we do not see his true motivation. The war appears to entice him as something of a novelty, and from this viewpoint Leper is to be pitied. His naiveté clouds his thinking and permits him to enter a cause for which he is vastly underprepared. He is an idealist, a loner, who has always sought pleasure in nature — in things that are beautiful and unmarred by destruction. Trees and beaver dams are far removed from the blood and gore of war.

Leper opens up the Devon community to a world beyond. For the most part we have seen life from the prep school standpoint — a sheltered, private existence that bears little resemblance to the war in progress. Leper is the link between civilization and inhumanity. His very departure shocks the students so much that they are barely able to discuss him.

Given the backdrop of the war, we are not surprised to find the students depressed as the winter drags on. The dirty, dull grayness of the campus is relieved at the last moment by an ingenious scheme of Finny's — the Carnival. There are rules against such carnivals at Devon — but the boys decide to have one anyway. It comes as a moment of inspiration and achieves its effect in the typical, Finnian manner: the Carnival generates energy, enthusiasm, courage and outright daring.

The Carnival unleashes in Gene a feeling of joy, exuberance and freedom. He experiences an inner peace he has never felt before. He is proud to be a budding athlete, happy about his new relationship with Finny, and overjoyed at the zesty playfulness of the Devon students at the Carnival. They are a group apart, an assembly of select individuals who have come together to celebrate life and ignore its woes. For this reason, Gene can now stand back and marvel at the event of the Carnival. It is an afternoon of "momentary, illusory, special and separate peace." The novel's title, then, refers to the emotion that Gene isolates from all other emotions in his life. For a brief moment, nothing is wrong, no one is hurt and life has meaning. Gene feels peace from within. Since he is distant from the turmoil that has led to this peace, he can enjoy the moment in a private, separate manner. He and Finny live apart from the world in their own separate peace.

But when Leper's telegram arrives, it shocks them out of this peace. They had begun the Carnival games by lighting a copy of Homer's *Iliad*, the great work about the Trojan War. Symbolically, they had initiated war games without paying much attention to the reality of war. Now that Leper has escaped from the war, they realize something of the war's true nature and lose touch with the "illusory peace" that had buoyed them earlier.

CHAPTER 10

Summary

Gene makes the trip to see his friend Leper. He knows that Leper is at home in Vermont because, in the telegram, Leper has stated, "I am at Christmas location." The journey between

Devon and Vermont is the first of many monotonous trips that Gene will take across an unknown countryside in the latter stages of the war. Though Gene is never to make it to the war, he nonetheless enlists in the army and is sent from one unknown settlement to another as part of the training process. This trip to Leper's home in Vermont later becomes associated in his mind with the army excursions.

He reaches the town at dawn and tries to understand what Leper meant by, "I have escaped." One doesn't "escape" the army, so Gene concludes that Leper must have escaped from some spies in the United States.

Approaching Leper's house, he sees the boy at the dining room window. Once inside, Gene follows Leper into the dining room and notices that Leper's lip twitches involuntarily, as though he were ready to snarl or cry. When Gene questions him about having escaped, Leper shouts angrily at him, "You're thinking I'm not normal, aren't you? . . . You're thinking I'm psycho."

This alarms Gene because he knows the army has done this to Leper. This is not the way Leper used to be.

Leper explains that the army was going to give him a dishonorable discharge — a Section Eight discharge, which is for "the nuts in the service, the psychos, the Funny Farm candidates." He knows that he would never be able to obtain a job with that kind of discharge. People would always look at him as if he were truly crazy.

They argue a bit because Gene tells him to stop yelling. Leper states that he always knew Gene was a savage underneath, "like that time you knocked Finny out of the tree . . . Like that time you crippled him for life." Gene stands up instantly and knocks Leper out of his chair. Mrs. Lepellier enters and sees what is happening. She is alarmed and asks Gene if he has come to abuse her son, who is ill.

But Leper is chuckling through his tears and crazed laughter, and asks Gene to stay for lunch. Gene accepts, simply because he is too ashamed to leave. Leper eats very little, but Gene wolfs down an enormous meal. This pleases Mrs. Lepellier, who becomes reconciled to him.

After lunch, the two boys take a walk. Leper says that in the army, he was considered to be "nervous": "nervous in the service." Gene replies that this sounds like one of Brinker's poems and, at this, Leper flies into a rage about Brinker. The fact that the latter has changed is of no interest to Leper: "I'd know that bastard if he'd changed into Snow White . . . Snow White with Brinker's face on her. There's a picture." Then he breaks into sobs.

Leper settles down and explains to Gene some of the hallucinations he has had: an arm of a chair turning into a person's arm, a man's body with a woman's head. These and other images reveal that Leper has partially lost touch with reality. He concludes that he is indeed "psycho," that the army always has the correct word for everything.

One day, he was looking at the corporal's face and couldn't determine who the man was. His face kept changing into faces of other people. "Then I began to think he looked like me, and then he . . . he changed into a woman." Caught up in the horror of his memories, Leper goes on to say more. But Gene has had enough and orders him to shut up. "Do you think I want to hear every gory detail! Shut up! I don't care! I don't care what happened to you, Leper. I don't give a damn! . . . . This has nothing to do with me!"

Gene takes off across the field, leaving Leper behind to tell his story to the wind. Gene wants no more of Leper's agonies, ever again.

Commentary

The chapter is simple and complicated at the same time. Structurally it concerns one event: the narration of Leper's tragic experience in the army and Gene's adverse reaction to it. But on a deeper level, it chronicles the wounds suffered by a sensitive young man induced too soon into the very adult world of war. Leper is not, by nature, suited to war. He has always been a peaceful, kind person, thrilled with the study of nature. To endure agony and authority every day is too much for his sensitive personality. When he reaches the breaking point, he fears that he would never recover from the damage of being labeled "psycho" and feels anguish at the idea of being so rejected. It would damn him for the rest of his life.

Gene, on the other hand, shows a complex reaction to Leper's horror. He is human enough to make the trip up to Vermont in an effort to help his friend. Yet he is too inexperienced with the realities of emotional trauma to be of any real assistance.

His final denial of Leper's tragedy (by turning his back and running away), comes as the ultimate insult to the young frail Leper, who is left behind, alone in a field of snow.

This chapter serves the major purpose of jolting us out of the "separate peace" of Gene's insulated world, and thrusting us (and Gene) into the more sordid reality of the wartime world. Leper's name takes on its full symbolic value in this chapter. Like a leper, he is ostracized by both the army and society. Alienated, he takes refuge in the privacy of his own boundless torment. We might say that if Finny and Gene experience their separate peace at the Carnival, then Leper now battles out a separate war — one which only he can combat and which only he can understand in its entirety.

CHAPTER 11

Summary
Gene wants to see Finny desperately. Upon arrival at Devon, he finds his friend throwing snowballs at a place called the Fields Beyond, an open ground past the gym, tennis courts and river. No one asks about Leper, except Finny — and even that is only brief curiosity. Gene stalls, preferring to deal with the question later.

The snowball fight continues, with participants changing sides regularly, until finally everyone gangs up on Finny. Of course Finny always admires energy, so he finds the fight riveting. Gene's only concern is that Finny ought to be careful not to fall. Dr. Stanpole has warned against this.

Back in their room that night, Gene notices the pictures that he and Finny have taped to the walls by their beds. Finny's picture shows the Roosevelt-Churchill meeting. Gene has photos which amount to a lie about his background: "weepingly romantic views of plantation mansions, moss-hung trees by moonlight, lazy roads winding dustily past the cabins of the Negroes." But he no longer needs this fictitious background to shore up his self-image; he feels himself becoming stronger and more self-confident.

When Finny asks about Leper, Gene decides to reveal the truth. "Leper is 'Absent Without Leave,' he just took off by himself." Finny and Brinker are horrified. Brinker suggests that Leper must be out of his mind. He adds that now two of the

Devon students are sidelined for the Duration. When Gene questions this statement, Brinker states that Phineas is also out of action. Finny agrees, but his remark that "there isn't any war" is now ironic. With that, all of his special inventions and fantasies die, leaving him and Gene in cold reality.

The campus is busy with recruiters and each day there are announcements about various training programs available to the students. For some reason, Gene chooses not to make a decision about the military. "I didn't feel free to, and I didn't know why this was so." Brinker accuses him of putting off the decision because of pity for Finny. Brinker is tired of people avoiding the issue of Finny's handicap and feels it is time to talk openly about it. He tells Gene that "it wouldn't do you any harm, you know, if everything about Finny's accident was cleared up and forgotten."

One evening, Finny takes up the topic of Leper. He realizes that Leper had been a gentle person and that the war must truly exist if it is capable of ruining someone real, like Leper.

Finny had seen Leper on campus that morning. Leper looked at him as if he were a gorilla and then ducked into someone's office. Finny and Gene burst out laughing because they are at a loss for words. Gene adds that he prefers Finny's notion that there is no war, to the sad reality of war.

At 10:05 that night, Brinker and three cohorts barge into Gene's room and announce that they are taking him out. He and Finny are lifted from their chairs and hustled down the stairs. They are transported to the First Building and, once inside, led to the Assembly Room. About ten members of the senior class are sitting on the platform, wearing their black graduation robes.

Brinker loudly draws their attention to Finny's limp. Then Gene and Finny are instructed to sit in the front row, where eight or ten others are already seated.

After reciting a prayer, Brinker addresses the issue of Finny's accident. He adds that it is time to clear up the mystery and suspicions surrounding the mishap. But Finny fails to understand and grows furious at the convocation. The line of questioning becomes heated, as various members demand to know exactly what happened that day. Gene is reluctant to reveal much, but Finny explains that he had been alone in the tree, with Gene below on the ground. Then Finny recalls, as if someone has suddenly slapped him in the face, that Gene and he had decided to make a double jump. They were both in the tree when the accident occurred.

Someone reports that Leper was present at the accident and might shed light on it. So they send for him, knowing that he is on campus that day. Leper enters the room moments later, clear-headed, bright and full of energy. He tells how he had seen both Finny and Gene high up in the tree together, that one of them was out on the limb while the other was close to the trunk, holding on for balance.

When Brinker asks Leper which boy shook the limb, Leper refuses to comment any further. "I don't intend to implicate myself. . . . I know when I have information that might be dangerous."

Finny wants no more of this. So he gets up and begins to leave. Gene rushes after him, but Finny turns and says, "I don't care . . . I just don't care. Never mind." When Brinker yells that they have not obtained all the facts, Finny turns with tears in his eyes and furiously dismisses their efforts. He rushes out of the room. As he starts down the stairs, he slips and falls. Everyone hears the noise of Finny's body "falling clumsily down the white marble stairs."

Commentary

This chapter has to do with coming of age, maturing into adulthood and making decisions that affect the outcome of one's future.

Gene feels a growing maturity and an increased sense of self-esteem. In his dorm room he has hung photos of Southern plantations and a romanticized way of life. Now, he realizes that he has attempted in the past to create a certain image for himself — an image meant to impress other people. With the return of Finny and the advances made in his athletic prowess, Gene has moved into a framework of greater self-confidence. "I no longer needed this vivid false identity; now I was acquiring, I felt, a sense of my own real authority and worth. I had had many new experiences and I was growing up."

This does not mean, however, that he does not still have some very deep feelings for Finny, or that their relationship has become less significant. It's just that Gene begins to identify some of the trivial events around him as part of the prep school atmosphere — an identification process that will have important repercussions. He and Finny discuss the war at length, but it is only after Gene's visit to Leper that they begin to see what is really happening in the world. That the war could affect someone as profoundly as it has affected Leper, disturbs the two boys very much. They are forced to conclude that there is indeed a war and that its effects are wide-ranging.

When the two of them laugh about Leper, it is not because of anything humorous. Rather, it is the release of uneasiness which neither knows how to express appropriately. Leper's experience is quite extraordinary, especially for someone of his age, and the boys know nothing about the need for sensitivity in these areas.

Brinker represents the establishment, and particularly that aspect of the establishment that prides itself on exercising authority over others. When he learns of Leper's catastrophe, Brinker's reaction is immediate. "He must be out of his mind . . . to do a thing like that. I'll bet he cracked up, didn't he?" This is the exact reaction that Leper predicted he would hear from most people. In fact, this premonition explains some of the force of his anxiety. He knew he was in for trouble, but there was nothing he could do about it. He was unprepared for the rigors of war, yet he now faces the prospect of future rejection in society.

Brinker is a budding bureaucrat who worships his own law. He hears only his own words and imposes his rigid values upon everyone nearby. It never occurs to Brinker — or those like him — that there are appalling circumstances associated with Leper's downfall and that the boy requires considerable sympathy and understanding. The Brinkers of the world — and we all know them — are always there when we least desire them, and they tend to be unusually prompt in their cold-hearted selfishness.

The chapter shows Finny at the peak of his turmoil. He knows now that he can no longer deny the war, even if he never really did so in his mind. He admits to Gene that the war is real and it is this confrontation with reality that changes their relationship. It shifts from fantasy and illusion to down-to-earth facts. Gene maintains some of Finny's characteristics ("I felt my face grimacing in the way Finny's did when he was really irritated"), yet he has developed traits of his own that distinguish him from his friend.

The only item that still divides them is the truth about what happened in the tree. Gene has attempted to explain himself to Finny (at Finny's home in Boston), but has not managed to do so. So when Brinker drags them off to the hearing in the First Building, Gene dreads the worst. It becomes a seamy ordeal in which students begin interrogating their peers, yet Brinker is determined to force the truth — or at least a version of the truth that will satisfy his need for openness.

Gene realizes that he cannot say too much. This would seem defensive, and he prefers to let others argue in his favor. He knows that if Finny accepts the truth about Gene's involvement in the accident, their friendship must end. Finny reaches a moment of clarity in which he understands, perhaps, that Gene caused the accident. But he shuts this out completely, opting to leave the room and abandoning all attempts to pursue the matter.

Finny accepts the fact that there really is a war. And it is likely that he also accepts the idea that Gene was involved in the accident. Until now, he has denied both. Now he sees the reality. He cannot join the army because of his physical condition, and there is nothing he can do to negate the occurrence of his accident. So, true to his optimistic nature, he chooses to move on with his life, leaving the ugliness behind.

Finny emerges from the meeting as something of a hero. He is grand in his desire to protect his friend Gene, and he shows courage in his attempts to rise above the pain of his fall. He does not wish to dwell on negative thoughts or to point a finger at victims. He tells Gene frequently that he believes in him. He knows that it is not possible to believe in everything or everyone in life, but he is comfortable with his friend. This is all that counts for him. It is more important than algebra, Latin or even the position of Gene in the tree the day of the fall.

Finny's fall down the stairs of the Assembly Hall is even more serious than his fall from the tree. It is Brinker and the inquisitors who have brought about this new tragedy. They are the ones anxious to prosecute Gene Forrester, yet they become the perpetrators of an even greater crime. If Gene can be blamed for causing Finny's broken leg, then Brinker and his pals are responsible for driving Finny to his death.

Depending upon one's point of view, there are numerous ways of looking at this. One might agree with Brinker that it was necessary to strive for "justice" at all costs, even if it meant harming another individual in the process. Or one might decide that Brinker had no right to interfere in Finny and Gene's relationship, that only these two should answer to one another. Regardless of one's position on the matter, the "enquiry" does not bring peace. Finny's private war with his physical ailment is almost over, as is his struggle to become involved in World War II. Since there is no possibility of his joining any army, and since he will never be able to compete in the Olympics, Finny has no purpose left in life. He is ready to die.

CHAPTER 12

Summary

Everyone behaves with "complete presence of mind" after Finny's fall. They do not move him, and one student goes directly to Dr. Stanpole's home for assistance. Phil Latham, the wrestling coach and an expert in first aid, wraps Finny in a blanket. Dr. Stanpole arrives and diagnoses the problem as another leg fracture, only this one is much cleaner than the last.

Finny is driven off in the doctor's car and Gene goes out into the night, pacing through the shadows. He spies Dr. Stanpole's car and considers stealing it. But the act strikes him as foolish so he abandons it.

He arrives at the window of the Infirmary, where Finny is being treated. He can hear "blurred voices droning monotonously through the window. If they do nothing worse, they're going to bore Finny to death." The night nurse has a reputation for being "the biggest windbag in the school, Miss Windbag, R.N." And Phil Latham, also present in the Infirmary, almost never speaks. One of the few things he has ever said is, "Give it the old college try" and Gene supposes that Finny is probably hearing this right now. Gene surmises that Finny will probably answer them in Latin.

This amuses Gene as he stands shivering, alone by the window. "I nearly laughed out loud at that. *Gallia est omnis divisa in partes tres* — Finny probably answered that whenever Phil Latham spoke." But when Gene puts his hand to his face, he feels tears. He has been crying, not laughing, and is almost out of control.

Dr. Stanpole leaves and the light is put out in Finny's

room. So Gene hoists the window open and calls to his friend. Finny lashes out at him with, "You want to break something else in me! Is that why you're here!" Finny struggles to attack Gene, but is unable to get out of bed. Finally "he brought his head slowly down between his hands and rested it against the floor, not moving, not making any sound."

Gene apologizes to him, over and over. He has enough control to refrain from entering Finny's room. He wanders aimlessly down a road and sees a double vision of the gym. Gene spends the night under a ramp beneath the stadium.

The next morning, he walks back to his room and finds a note tacked to his door. It is from Dr. Stanpole, asking Gene to bring some of Finny's clothes to the Infirmary. Gene does not look forward to seeing Finny, but nonetheless dutifully takes his clothes over. When he enters Finny's room, his friend instructs him to place the suitcase on the bed. Finny's voice is very matter-of-fact. It is neither friendly nor unfriendly, "not interested and not bored, not energetic and not languid."

Gene feels powerless and extremely uncomfortable, wanting to flee but remaining trapped. He notices finally that Finny's hands are shaking, so he breaks the silence with, "Finny, I tried to tell you before, I tried to tell you when I came to Boston that time—" Finny is quick to understand and becomes more compassionate. But within moments he slams his fist into the suitcase and screams, "I wish to God there wasn't any war . . . What good are you in a war with a busted leg!"

He confesses to Gene that he has written to "the Army and the Navy and the Marines and the Canadians and everybody else all winter." Though Finny is desperate to serve in the military, no one will accept him. His physical condition makes him ineligible.

Gene cuts him off by saying that Finny would have been no good at war, even if he hadn't ruined his leg. Finny would have made friends with the enemy, arranged games with them and thoroughly confused everybody. "You'd make a mess, a terrible mess, Finny, out of the war."

Finny is crying and wondering if Gene had felt a blind impulse in the tree, when the accident occurred. He wants to believe that Gene didn't know what he was doing, and Gene quickly acknowledges this to be true. Finny believes his friend. "It wasn't anything you really felt against me, it wasn't some kind of hate you've felt all along. It wasn't anything personal." Gene confirms this.

Finny believes him and peace descends on them both. Dr. Stanpole has said he was going to set Finny's bone that afternoon, and that Gene could come by at five o'clock to see him. The rest of the day passes uneventfully. At 4:45 Gene goes to the Infirmary and sits on a bench in the hall. Ten minutes later, Dr. Stanpole walks rapidly down the hall toward him. He sits beside Gene and announces, "This is something I think boys of your generation are going to see a lot of . . . and I will have to tell you about it now. Your friend is dead."

In the middle of the operation, some marrow had apparently escaped from the bone and gone directly to Finny's heart.

Gene does not cry "then or ever about Finny. I did not cry even when I stood watching him being lowered into his family's straight-laced burial ground outside of Boston. I could not escape a feeling that this was my own funeral, and you do not cry in that case."

Commentary

This is the chapter toward which the entire novel has been building. It is, for many readers, a sad, disturbing chapter that prompts reactions ranging from disbelief to anger. Perhaps the various reactions parallel those we experience in life when someone we know dies. But one thing is sure: the chapter never fails to provoke some type of feeling from deep inside.

Gene and Finny have grown close — much closer than many roommates, and in a way that goes beyond mere friendship. They have come to need each other, and depend on certain characteristics of one another that they cannot find elsewhere. They satisfy and fulfill various mutual needs, but at the same time they rebuff and alienate each other. They want, but do not want, the other's friendship. They need (but have trouble admitting this) to extend themselves in the form of the other person.

So when Finny falls on the stairs, it brings to a head many emotions that have been building for some time — emotions from the deep world of lurking fear, anger and unpredictable violence. Gene has for a long time felt left out of the athletic world dominated by Finny. He has always known that Finny was brilliant and special, and he has felt the impulses of attraction to him without being able to resist. Whether he liked it or not, he was magnetized by Finny.

On the other hand, Finny feels left out of Gene's life after the accident. He sees the normal, healthy body of his friend and regrets his own disability. He is deprived of ever fulfilling certain dreams — such as getting involved in the war or competing in the Olympic Games — and he seeks fulfillment in vicarious ways, by living through Gene.

The two, then, have at various times in their friendship felt prevented by circumstance from fully enjoying life. They have wanted to possess each other's superior traits. But, more importantly, they have also needed these traits for self-definition. So, when Finny is carried to the Infirmary, Gene says,

> He went past with his eyes closed and his mouth tense. I knew that normally I would have been one of those carrying the chair, saying something into his ear as we went along. My aid alone had never seemed to him in the category of help. The reason for this occurred to me as the procession moved slowly across the brilliant foyer to the doors: Phineas had thought of me as an extension of himself."

Finny's character before the accident bears little resemblance to the one we see afterward. Likewise with Gene. He is a different person after the fall, much closer to being a man, to being forced into an internal debate about life's responsibilities.

When Finny falls down the stairs, Gene remains detached from the action. He does not wish to stand beside his friend because he fears an outburst of anger from him. It is the tragic moment of seeing a loved one being carried off by strangers, and not being able to help in any way.

They are extensions of one another, and yet still separated by the truth concerning the fall from the tree. If the accident had never occurred, Finny would never have been disabled on the marble steps, nor would this late-night meeting at the First Building ever have taken place. The second fall derives from the first one, and Finny's anger originated at the scene of that initial accident. To break a limb is one thing. But to break one's life is something quite different. This is what the first fall did to Finny; it broke his life. It prevented him from living the kind of life he had always led and from developing into the sort of man he was destined to be.

Finny is leery of Gene. Whether by coincidence or strategy, Gene has been present at both these accidents. So something inside prompts Finny to wonder about Gene's role in them. When Gene finally gets Finny's attention in the Infirmary, the night of the staircase accident, Finny responds with, "You want to break something else in me! Is that why you're here!" By this point, Finny feels that life has failed him and his body has betrayed him. Not only is he an invalid, but his sense of worth has collapsed. No wonder Gene's presence comes as little solace to him.

But there is more. There is some measure of truth in the saying that one hurts most the people one loves. Finny indicates, in this statement, that all pretense and facade are gone. He reveals truthfully the thought on his mind, regardless of its hurtful impact on Gene. His survival is at stake and he cannot play games any longer.

So the comment, while it stabs Gene, is made in total truthfulness. Yet when the two boys meet the next day, this "truthfulness" paves the way for even greater intimacy. The dream of their friendship — the fantasies and illusions and aspirations — has merged with reality and there is no separating the two.

Finny has waged war on life in his incapacitated state and has lost. Like a war veteran, he is carted off to the Infirmary and eventually dies. His death is disturbing for more than one reason. It is somehow unbelievable in the context, a little too convenient for the novelist's purposes. It would have had much greater impact to leave Finny alive, but to orient him toward a disabled future for which Gene would always feel responsible.

Finny wants desperately to be involved in the war. War means action, and action involves human effort. Finny has excelled at this, before the accident, and wants ways of proving to himself that he is still vibrant. He says,

> I'll *hate* it *everywhere* if I'm not in this war! Why do you think I kept saying there wasn't any war all winter? I was going to keep on saying it until two seconds after I got a letter from Ottawa or Chungking or some place saying, 'Yes, you can enlist with us.'

Finny views rejection from the army as being a rejection from life, from activity.

Thus, the two boys are miserable for different reasons: Gene regrets the cause, and Finny regrets the effect. They both deplore the outcome of the original accident and would like to change things. But failing this, they come to accept one another and to abide by the truth. Finny accepts Gene's explanation about the impulsiveness of the act (jiggling the tree branch), and Gene realizes that he has finally made peace with his best friend. Again, it is a peace that only they share, in the privacy of Finny's room. It is, once again, a very separate peace.

And so is the peace that lingers after Finny's death. It is not a peace of contentment or joy or satisfaction, but a peace of neutrality, emptiness and finality. If Gene does not cry when Finny's body is lowered into the ground, it is because there are no more tears to shed. Gene too has suffered death. His alter ego, best friend and constant source of energy has been taken away, replaced by nothing. The only thing left for Gene to do is live the way Finny would have wanted him to live. The obvious path of action is to enlist in the army.

CHAPTER 13

Summary
The Far Common on the Devon campus has been donated to the war effort. In early June, Gene stands at his window and watches as soldiers move in to occupy the Far Common. The troops "were not very bellicose-looking; their columns were straggling, their suntan uniforms had gotten rumpled in the train, and they were singing *Roll Out the Barrel*." The trucks contain sewing machines and Brinker suggests that Leper would have been all right if he had joined the Army Air Force. Gene cuts him off, preferring not to discuss "something you can't do anything about."

Gene feels it is pointless to talk about things one can't change. He is grateful that no one accuses him of being responsible for Phineas's death.

Brinker's father arrives and Gene is introduced to him. "He was a distinguished-looking man, taller than Brinker . . . His hair was white, thick, and healthy-looking and his face was healthily pink." Mr. Hadley scoffs at the G.I.'s with sewing machines. In his day, a man would never have settled for such ridicule. He asks which branch of the military Gene intends to enlist in and Gene replies that he was going to wait until he was drafted. But then he had decided that if he did this, he would surely be placed in the infantry, the dirtiest and most dangerous branch of all. So he has joined the Navy and will be sent to Pensacola.

Gene adds that Brinker intends to join the Coast Guard. This causes Mr. Hadley to frown disappointedly at his son. He wants Brinker to see lots of action, to participate heroically and honorably in the war effort. Coast Guard work is too "comfortable." Mr. Hadley feels obliged to explain that his son should be sure he is making the correct decisions. "Your war memories will be with you forever, you'll be asked about them thousands of times after the war is over." He believes that the boys should not pay attention to which jobs are dirty or difficult. They should strive for action at the front so that they can boast, in years to come, about their bravery.

His father's oratory about serving one's country embarrasses Brinker more than Gene. Brinker argues that his father's generation is responsible for the war that they, Brinker and *his* generation, will have to fight. Gene disagrees. He believes "that wars were not made by generations and their special stupidities, but that wars were made instead by something ignorant in the human heart."

Gene walks over to the gym to clean out his locker. On the way, he notices that the campus is already being transformed into a place he fails to recognize. Though he had once been happy at Devon, "such times it seemed to me . . . were over now. Happiness had disappeared along with rubber, silk, and many other staples, to be replaced by wartime synthetic, high morale, for the Duration."

Gene never talks about Finny. Nor does anyone else. "He was, however, present in every moment of every day since Dr. Stanpole had told me. Finny had a vitality which could not be quenched so suddenly, even by the marrow of his bone."

Through death, Finny has escaped the war. He died a harmonious and natural human being. As Gene prepares to depart from Devon, with diploma in hand, he knows that his formal education is over. The military lies ahead for him but Gene isn't fazed at all. "I was ready for the war, now that I no longer had any hatred to contribute to it. My fury was gone, I felt it gone, dried up at the source, withered and lifeless. Phineas had absorbed it and taken it with him, and I was rid of it forever.''

He never will kill anyone, nor does he ever develop an intense hatred for the enemy. ''Because my war ended before I ever put on a uniform; I was on active duty all my time at school; I killed my enemy there.''

Commentary

This final chapter is one of retrospection and self-evaluation. Gene knows that he has come a long way since his initial days at Devon and his deep friendship with Finny. He knows also that Finny has not died; he has merely passed out of his body. The spirit of Finny remains everywhere within Gene's universe. It is a source of energy, truth, and fearlessness.

The two have been intertwined for much of the novel. Now that they are separated, we see a new Gene emerge. He has grown beyond his fears, put them in the past, and assessed himself alongside his school companions. All of them — Brinker, Leper, Quackenbush, and even the teacher Mr. Ludsbury — have been afraid of something and have constructed elaborate defenses to protect themselves against their fears. Yet these fears of an enemy have been unnecessary. As is often the case, the enemy never really existed. It has been a fantasy, a contorted obsession that has filled their minds with negativity and paralyzed them against more positive action.

Finny was not victimized by such fears. He alone feared nothing and no one. From him, Gene learns tranquillity and peace of mind. This is why he is fearless about entering the armed services. When Gene states that he killed his enemy at Devon, he refers to the dual enemy against which he had been battling: Finny and himself — Finny, because Finny represented a force over which Gene had little control, and himself, because Gene was not comfortable with his fears, insecurities, jealousies, resentments and aspirations.

Finny taught Gene how to examine life from a truthful, factual standpoint. Fiction and dalliance, while part of Finny's playfulness, had little role in his ultimate decisions about things. Gene is now able to benefit from that attitude. He looks only at what seems real about life, ''letting its rocklike facts sift through.'' He makes no attempt to shut Finny out of his mind, but rather tells himself truth and fact about the relationship.

The episode with Brinker's father serves to point out the vast differences between generations, which color our values. Mr. Hadley represents the old school while his son represents the new. It is an objective way of portraying change, of showing that ideas progress and evolve. This is what happened with Gene throughout the course of the novel, and it also happened to Finny, whose childlike nature, characterized by great energy and enthusiasm, is gradually transformed, becoming more mature and responsible. *A Separate Peace* ends on a positive, constructive note. But because of Gene's complicated interactions with Finny on a private, personal level, one wonders to what extent his pain does not continue into the next, unwritten chapter.

Character Sketches

Gene Forrester

Gene is the narrator of the novel. Without him, there would be no purpose for telling the story of *A Separate Peace*. The story, which tells of an intensely emotional and intellectual grappling for internal peace, is the chronologically narrated tale of Gene's relationship with his friend Finny. We enter the novel fifteen years after the incidents of the story actually take place. Gene, as the narrator, highlights the important points of his time at Devon.

Gene comes from the South to attend Devon School in the Northeast. Immediately the beliefs and values of these two regions are set in opposition. As a southerner, Gene arrives in New Hampshire with a parcel of values inculcated by his family — pride for the southland, a sense of superiority and honor associated with his family ancestry, eagerness to boast of his southern-mansion background. But we realize that much of this is false — that Gene's sensitivities prohibit him from believing in the values he displays on the surface. Beneath the veneer, he is deeply committed to finding the truth, to discovering what it is about life that creates meaning and purpose.

Gene has been conditioned to keep his beliefs to himself: it is better to present a polite, consenting facade, even if deep inside there is violent disagreement with a situation. This manner is very common in the South, where gentility and romance have long prevailed in both mythology and reality. While there are obvious exceptions, it remains true that southerners see themselves as better mannered than their northern counterparts.

But keeping one's thoughts and feelings inside can lead only to smoldering resentment and anger. So when Gene comes into contact with the spry, free-living Finny, whose northern outlook on life differs radically from Gene's, there are serious consequences. Gene suppresses anger and resentment, goes along with his roommate's ideas, allows himself to be led into activities that he might otherwise have shunned, and, at a critical moment, finds himself releasing his resentment in a symbolic act of fury. By causing Finny to fall, Gene fulfills his suppressed urge to destroy his friend. Revenge and justice are two very important ideals of the American South.

But it would be unfitting to describe Gene as vengeful or

violent. He is an honest, well-meaning young man who is anxious to please, to fit in with the crowd and achieve in areas where he has talent. He enjoys his schoolwork, excels at it when he takes it seriously and is respected by his colleagues. Gene is often bitter, unhappy and depressed, but just as often he is delighted and fanciful. The combination makes for an intense, complex set of feelings.

Gene undergoes considerable character growth in the novel. He emerges from a sort of shyness into a more confident posture. He learns about people and events and life in a way he might never have imagined possible, had he not been influenced by Finny. He is sensitive toward others and finds pleasure in the bond of his relationship with Finny. The two are inseparable, even through the apparent crises of hostility and enmity. Gene values Finny more than any other person in his life. Finny becomes like a brother to him. Yet their relationship treads a thin line between many opposing emotions, including anger, sadness, jubilation, fantasy and even sexuality, in a deeply unconscious manner.

Gene must be seen as the alter ego of Finny. They complement one another remarkably well. When Gene is conservative, Finny is liberal. When the former is reluctant, the latter is rambunctious. When one is apathetic, the other brims with energy. Therefore we must attempt to see Gene not only as an individual who achieves peace, but as one who is, was, and always will be inextricably interwoven with the personality of his friend Finny. In short, Gene needs Finny in order to realize himself. His fulfillment as a human being depends entirely on the lessons learned at Devon. He travels the full circle of emotion and achieves inner peace only through this process.

Phineas (Finny)

Finny is energy personified. He moves, thinks and lives spontaneously, with no trace of pretense, pomp or conceit. He is a natural being, one who fascinates by sheer force. He magnetizes all those in his presence and delights in provoking controversy. He sparks energy wherever he goes and succeeds in attracting followers from every corner.

Finny excels in sports and, more generally, in all physical activity. He is natively shrewd and creative — very much an entrepreneur — yet he shows little interest in the organized form of scholarship. Finny prefers to learn as he goes rather than to sit down and memorize. He is not a thinker as much as he is an originator. When he becomes involved in something, he goes wholeheartedly at his task, reveling in the inventiveness and plunging new meaning into every chosen moment.

With his blitzball game, he invents rules as he progresses, slowly evolving a game that catches on wildly with the students. Through Gene's regimen of jogging, Finny devotes himself selflessly to the purpose of improving his friend's athletic agility. Finny is an ingenious and colorful original whose like is rare and whose importance extends in innumerable directions.

If we take his fall from the tree as a symbol of something larger — as some have done in comparing this episode to the fall from Eden — then we see a Finny who copes equally well with the pleasures of paradise and the vicissitudes of sin. He adjusts to his handicap and strives to succeed in ways that otherwise might not have occurred to him.

Finny has a need to control his surroundings, and this is what ultimately does him in. When he falls from the tree, it is his first incident of physical clumsiness. He does not cause the fall; he cannot control it. His native finesse is unable to prevail when he is caught off guard.

Finny grows to need Gene as much as the latter needs him. Their needs are, of course, different yet complementary. Finny needs Gene's mental power and ability to withstand discipline. And Gene is fascinated by Finny's spontaneity and grace, his inquisitiveness and inspiration.

Leper Lepellier

Leper is one of the great tragedies of this novel. He is a gentle boy given to curiosity about nature's secrets. His snails, beavers and other interests reveal him as one who would never harm anyone. Yet it is this very sensitivity that damns him in the army. He is unable to withstand the brutality with which military life bludgeons the personality. It is a shock to him that human beings can crunch into one another in such violent, unpeaceful ways. So he is faced with a choice: to stay in the service and be discharged as a "psycho" (since he has lost his ability to act rationally) or to flee the scene of the trauma. He chooses the latter.

Leper maintains his dignity despite this catastrophe in his

life. He is moved to tears, yet he honors Gene's right to justice in the mock trial held by Brinker Hadley. Leper is, in this regard, both the weakest and the strongest character in the novel. He has been hurt, yet he wishes not to hurt others. Therein lies his immense likability.

· Brinker Hadley

Brinker is the class show-off, the proud young aristocrat whose background has prepared him for an honorable life as a cigar puffer and billiard parlor inhabitant. He shows promise as a leader, both locally and at Devon School, yet fluctuates between his duty to serve the country and his desire to remain alive. He is the son of an arrogant man whose pride rests in being able to brag about his past military glories, even if many of them are purely fictitious. Brinker is something of a bore, especially when he imposes his untested opinions as facts. He becomes horrifying, as a young radical capable of right-wing persecution politics tinged with nazi overtones.

He is one of the brightest in his class, yet lives in the shadow of a dominating family. Brinker veers from the path of glory and power in order to assert himself finally as a candidate for the Coast Guard.

Critical Appraisal

In the last chapter of *A Separate Peace* the war moves into the quadrangles of the Devon School. During the innocent summer of 1942, it was unreal; during the "illusory, special and separate peace" that Finny managed to maintain during the winter of 1943, it was inexorably drawing nearer, and in Leper's collapse it became a fearful reality.

But as the jeeps roll in behind the unheroic truckloads of sewing machines, the face of war that Leper saw is modified by another: the war also turns out to be a prosaic business without horror and without glory, to which, Gene says, "I no longer had any hatred to contribute."

When Gene rejects Brinker's outburst against his father's generation along with Finny's comic version of the same complaint, it is because he has come to a conclusion of his own about war:

> I could never agree with either of them. It would have been comfortable, but I could not believe it. Because it seemed clear that wars were not made by generations and their special stupidities, but that wars were made instead by something ignorant in the human heart.

If we pay attention to this, we will not misunderstand what Gene says a few pages later, after telling us of his inability to use the past tense about Phineas. "During the time I was with him, Phineas created an atmosphere in which I continued now to live," and when Gene goes to war, he says, "I fell into step as well as my nature, Phineas-filled, would allow."

> I never killed anybody and I never developed an intense level of hatred for the enemy. Because my war ended before I ever put on a uniform; I was on active duty all my time at school; I killed my enemy there.

Some readers have thought that Gene is talking about Phineas here. It is not Phineas, but the "something ignorant" in his heart that Gene has recognized as his enemy and killed. His war was with himself and is now ended.

But if Phineas was not the enemy, who was he, and what is his role in Gene's war?

The Rational and Instinctive Selves

That both boys are athletes is an important factor in the story. Gene first discovers evil in himself through physical action. Almost everything Gene has ever done, until that moment in the tree with Finny, has been controlled and thought out.

But during the following winter, Gene makes a further discovery about himself, again revealed through physical exertion. One morning Gene is labouriously and painfully running laps under Finny's supervision. In the moment before he is released from his imprisonment in dogged, conscious effort, Gene's "head felt as though different sections of the cranium were grinding each other."

> Then, for no reason at all, I felt magnificent. It was as though my body until that instant had simply been lazy, as though the aches and exhaustion were all imagined, created from nothing in order to keep me from truly exerting myself. Now my body seemed at last to say, "Well, if you must have it, here!" and an accession of strength came flooding through me. Buoyed up, I forgot my usual feeling of routine self-pity when working out, I lost myself, oppressed mind along with aching body; all entanglements were shed, I broke into the clear.

Gene pulls up in front of Phineas, not even winded, and the following conversation takes place:

> "You found your rhythm, didn't you, that third time around. Just as you came into that straight part there."
>
> "Yes, right there."
>
> "You've been pretty lazy all along, haven't you?"
>
> "You didn't even know anything about yourself."
>
> "I don't guess I did, in a way."

67

"In a way," — because Gene has already been grappling with a dark self-knowledge acquired in the tree, when he also "lost himself" and, freed from fear as Finny fell to the ground, jumped into the river without thinking. In the first instance, he found that when released from the control of his conscious mind, he was capable of destructive violence. Now he learns, under Finny's continuing influence, that this is not all he is capable of when freed from "the dictates of my mind, which gave me the maneuverability of a strait-jacket." Gene has moved toward freeing himself from the fear of trusting his instincts.

Finny has never known this fear. But if he does not fear his instincts, Finny at least once refuses to listen to what they tell him. "I had a kind of feeling," Finny says in the hospital after the accident. "But you can't say anything for sure from just feelings," and he apologizes to Gene for "that feeling I had."

Gene has observed earlier that "Finny's life was ruled by inspiration and anarchy, and so he prized a set of rules. His own, not those imposed on him by other people, such as the faculty of Devon School." Finny is not a mere symbol of the anarchy of instinct any more than Gene is entirely "strait-jacketed" by his mind. There is an interchange of roles and a lifelike complexity in their behaviour.

The Lepellier Refusal

Besides Gene and Phineas, there is a third character who not only plays a decisive role in the final section of the book but whose personal disintegration throws an interesting light on Gene's own struggle.

Leper Lepellier, vague and timid, is an unnoticed presence at the foot of the tree when Finny falls, inconspicuous during the winter term except when his solitary skiing tour arouses Brinker's scorn, from which Gene feels an impulse to protect him.

On a first reading we may hardly notice, in the excitement of blitzball, the moment in which Gene passes the ball to Leper.

> Taken by surprise, Leper looked up in anguish, shrank away from the ball, and voiced his first thought, a typical one. "I don't want it."

Finny stops the game and invents on the spot a rule to cover this situation, to which he gives a significant name: The Lepellier Refusal. This may not immediately remind us of an earlier exchange between Gene and Phineas, on the way back from their first jump from the tree.

"You were very good," said Finny good-humouredly, "once I shamed you into it."

"You didn't shame anybody into anything."

"Oh yes I did. I'm good for you that way. You have a tendency to back away from things otherwise."

"I never backed away from anything in my life!" I cried, my indignation at this charge naturally stronger because it was so true.

There is a kinship in the refusal, or reluctance, of both Leper and Gene to face certain challenges that experience presents to them. As Leper's withdrawal is more extreme than Gene's, he is more devastated when his defenses fail him.

When Leper's telegram interrupts the Winter Carnival, summoning Gene not to the 1944 Olympics but to a confrontation with the horror Leper has discovered in the war and Leper's frightening judgment upon Gene himself, it is Gene's turn to resort to the Lepellier Refusal: *I don't want it.* "This has nothing to do with me!" Gene says.

This crucial tenth chapter is a remarkable piece of writing: from the ease and rightness with which the train ride becomes a metaphor for Gene's future war experience, to the bleak scene in the snow with the trees crackling like rifles as Gene beats a retreat from the ravings of the poor creature who had signed his telegram "Your best friend." In between, every detail of Gene's behaviour — his cautious small talk, his withdrawal into "a scornful superiority, based on nothing," his shame over his enormous appetite at lunch — commands belief and shamed recognition.

What Gene finally runs away from is the threat that what has happened to Leper can happen to him. Notice what Leper is saying when Gene decides he can't stand any more and cuts him off: that faces and things began to lose their real identity for him. "One day I couldn't make out what was happening to the corporal's face. It kept changing into faces I knew from somewhere else, and then I began to think he looked like me, and then he . . ." As Leper is saying this, his voice thickens "unrecognizably."

A few nights later, Gene suffers his own crisis of identity. Instead of things and faces losing their reality for him, they seem brilliantly real as he wanders across the schoolgrounds to the deserted stadium. Only he himself seems unreal and like a ghost,

> as though my whole life at Devon had been a dream, or rather that everything at Devon, the playing fields, the gym, the water hole, and all the other buildings and all the people there were intensely real, wildly alive and totally meaningful, and I alone was a dream, a figment which had never really touched anything . . . I did not exist.

This is Gene's lowest point. But he has done one thing tonight that will save him, and that was his trip to the window of Finny's hospital room, from which Finny furiously drove him away.

Gene's Salvation

The four-page scene in Finny's hospital room the following morning, rendered almost entirely in dialogue with little comment by Gene, is the culmination of the novel. If it had not taken place, it is possible that Gene might not have found his way back from the darkness in which he floundered the night before. What we are shown is that he performs a decisive act of courage, and is released from a condition of self-doubt and fear in which he might have walled himself up forever.

When he arrives at Finny's bedside, Gene is released from his initial speechless hesitation by noticing that Finny's hands are shaking; and when he finds at last the important thing he has to say, "My voice found that full tone voices have when they are expressing something long felt and long understood and released at last."

When Gene first realized, on the way to the tree, that Finny was not his enemy, he thought only of the shadow this cast on his own character: "I was not of the same quality as he." Now he loses all concern for himself, and in describing Finny's character to him, he says at last what he was unable to say to Finny on the beach: *You are my friend*.

In spite of what Gene has done to Finny, he has the simplicity to say, "I thought I belonged here," in answer to Finny's question of why he came to the window the night before. We remember that at the moment of Finny's declaration on the beach, Gene commented on Finny's courage in speaking his feelings. Gene finds that courage at last. In fact, what Gene does now is harder: if he was mistaken once in thinking Phineas his enemy, he has good reason to dread Finny's hatred now, when the terrible wrong he committed is no longer hidden. Gene's salvation is that he doesn't think of himself at all; he thinks of Finny. He notices Finny's hands trembling and he puts his feeling of Finny's essential quality into words.

Isn't this what Finny means, when in answer to Gene's "How can I show you?" Finny says, "You've already shown me and I believe you." Gene's behaviour has shown that his love for Finny is stronger than the momentary impulse in the tree.

Who is the Enemy?

Looking at a world at war in the light of his personal experience at Devon, Gene Forrester comes to believe that wars are made by an ignorance which leads us to mistake the natures of those around us and to fear enemies where — perhaps — none exist.

Examining his own behaviour and that of others at Devon — Mr. Ludsbury's, Brinker's, Quackenbush's, Leper's — Gene concludes that the "obsessive labour of defense" in personal life is the same impulse that betrays men into the group activity of war. In tracing the evil of war back to "something ignorant in the human heart," *A Separate Peace* invites comparison with another first novel of the 1950's, William Golding's *Lord of the Flies*. When asked by his American publishers for a statement of that book's purpose, Golding answered:

The theme is an attempt to trace the defects of society back to the defects of human nature. The moral is that the shape of a society must depend on the ethical nature of the individual and not on any political system however apparently logical and respectable.

The marooned boys in Golding's book fear attack by a Beast which may come up out of the water around their island, or down from a ridge they have not had the courage to explore. Only one of their number, Simon, suggests that "The beast may be us," but is unable to make clear to the others what he means by this.

Later Simon, left alone in a clearing with the pig's head offered up to the Beast, imagines that the head says to him:

> "Fancy thinking the Beast was something you could kill! . . . You knew, didn't you? I'm part of you? Close, close, close! I'm the reason why it's no go? Why things are what they are?"

Having discovered the true nature of the enemy, Simon wanders up to the ridge where the others thought they sighted the Beast and finds only the harmless dead body of a parachutist fallen from a plane like the boys themselves. But when he interrupts a mindless war dance of frightened boys, Simon himself is mistaken for the Beast and slaughtered before he can tell them of his discovery.

At the end of Golding's book, his central character Ralph weeps "for the end of innocence, the darkness of man's heart, and the fall through the air of the true, wise friend called Piggy," destroyed in the reversion to savagery that took place on the island. Ignorance and fear are enemies in both stories, but the two fables differ in their estimation of human potentiality to overcome evil. The Beast in Golding's story cannot be conquered; the veneer of civilized behaviour cracks to reveal an ungovernable destructive force. Leper's "You always were a savage underneath" is the statement of the evil in human nature against which the reasonable Ralph and Piggy and the murdered Simon are powerless.

But Leper's is not the final judgment of Gene's nature in *A Separate Peace*. Though Gene committed an act of savagery and Phineas died as an eventual result of it, the example of Phineas seems to suggest to Gene that the instinctual, spontaneous impulses of our nature need not be a source of evil, to be bottled up or crippled or killed, but can be accepted as Phineas accepted himself. Balance is a possibility, as Phineas balanced on the limb of the tree before Gene shook him off; and though Phineas himself is destroyed, the grace embodied in his brief life outlives him as an ideal of conduct.

Gene holds to the possibility that out of the wreckage of innocence, something survives. Phineas had "a heightened confidence in himself, a serene capacity for affection which saved him," and may save Gene.

John Knowles has argued, in his essay *A Protest from Paradise*, that a loss of paradisal happiness — like Gene Forrester's loss — may lie behind some novelists's efforts toward creating an image "to make the loss very much less than complete." To the examples he mentions, he might have added the testimony of Proust, who says something very similar at the end of his work. In Knowles' words:

> The perfect world they had known was overlaid, buried, smothered.
>
> It was not entirely lost however. It became a permanent assumption of theirs, a taken-for-granted feeling about the possibilities of life; a vision of what might somehow be . . .

So Phineas remains in Gene Forrester's mind as an image of "what might somehow be," as Gene enters manhood. Gene believes, as John Knowles does, in the possibilities of life.

Selected Criticisms

By means of the removed narrative perspective, the author makes the most of a story which has only a single dramatic incident. . . . Gene weaves into his narrative a series of schoolboy capers that have the charm of the F. Scott Fitzgerald of *"This Side of Paradise."* Oddly enough, some of these scenes have more novelistic appeal than the ugly central incident at the "jumping-tree". . . . The novel's final movement, one feels, is inevitable. Yet, when it takes place, it is without an accompanying sense of conclusiveness and significance — the hard core of reality upon which the final pages seem to depend.

Donald Yates, *Chicago Sunday Tribune* (March 27, 1960)

A cleanly, unobtrusively yet affectingly written first novel. . . . Mr. Knowles has written perceptively about both youth and the wartime climate in which his young people live.

Christian Century (June 8, 1960)

Original and arresting story. . . . Although Finny is never completely credible and although the mock trial at the end seems contrived, this book rates high indeed because of the directness of the writing, the authenticity of school setting, the absolute reality of the tensions, fears, almost unbearable exuberance these adolescents experience as they develop.

M.C. Scoggin, *Horn Book* (October 1960)

Mr. Knowles draws with tenderness and restraint the pure joy of affection between the boys, their laconic, conscientiously fantastic language and the extra tension of the summer — 1942 — when they see their youth curtailed by war. The book is small but substantial.

Anne Duchene, *Manchester Guardian* (May 1, 1959)

A consistently admirable exercise in the craft of fiction — disciplined, precise, witty and always completely conscious of intention and effect — and yet, in spite of these rare assets (or perhaps because of them), the novel's final effect is one of remoteness and aridity. . . . Having chosen a theme which echoes in every sensitive man's experience, Mr. Knowles chooses further to isolate it from the mainstream of life, almost as if he were examining one case of a disease which rages in an epidemic throughout the rest of the world. All that intelligence and industry, tact and talent can bring to his novel are here, but its virtues breed its defects as the story unfolds. . . . The force and briefness which might have charged *A Separate Peace* with an electric depth are diluted by the restrictions the author has chosen to impose upon his story (especially the deliberate exclusion of parents and backgrounds, as if boys arrive at school from a vacuum) and a somewhat cautious approach which insists upon gazing from a distance upon the seething cauldron of adolescent nature. It is we the readers who must provide the substance from our response to personal experience in similar relationships.

Hardin Lemay, New York Herald Tribune Book Review (March 6, 1960)

Mr. Knowles' book has great depth. Here we may read messages which only become clear much later, after we have pondered long over the disturbing allegories. The interpretation of the messages must be highly subjective, which holds true of all major works of art.

Douglas Aitken, San Francisco Chronicle (June 26, 1960)

A novel of altogether exceptional power and distinction. . . . Mr. Knowles's world is the real world where black-and-white character-contrasts rarely lie conveniently to hand. Gene and Finny can slip in and out of each other's roles and yet remain entirely themselves while doing so. Their relationship has that subtle elusiveness which is entirely human and which novelists, with good reason, find desperately difficult to convey.

The other characters — masters and boys — are all given life and individuality. The school itself, gradually losing something of its relaxed, patrician manner as the war draws closer, is described with precision and economy.

London Times Literary Supplement (May 1, 1959)

Review Questions and Answers

Question 1.

Discuss the theme of emotional development in *A Separate Peace*.

Answer

The presence of the war, in a sense, serves as a background for the emotional development of the young men at Devon. The war is a device associated with a heightened state of emotion and, in *A Separate Peace*, it triggers buried emotions in each of the characters. Sports at the school parallel the actual war as a more direct stimulus for emotional development. Gene, Finny and Brinker become very competitive. Finny's competitive instinct is channelled into sport until his first accident and, after that, he coaches Gene so that he can represent them both. Gene wavers between sports and his academic subjects, and his major effort ends in the field of studies, a decision reached due to his growth emotionally.

The two examples of strife, sports and war, become the keys to the emotional development of characters, particularly Gene, of whose emotions we are almost always aware. Each character, due to the uncertainty he feels, is virtually "at war" with himself. The inability to resolve, in some way, this inner conflict (seen so clearly in Gene's ever-changing feelings about Finny), seems to end in either death (Finny) or madness (Leper). Finny is unable to face certain feelings, which ends in his becoming upset at the trial, having a second accident and dying. Leper searches for a quick and artificial escape from his loneliness, and returns in worse shape than when he left. Gene, however, in a very painful process, remains at school and "fights it out" within himself. Friendship becomes the major field of competition, and the battle is a long one. The conflict he feels within himself, in his relationship to Finny, is the source of his final emotional development. Due to the "accident" which he caused, he is forced to examine his feelings over and over again throughout the novel. This intensive and unpleasantly painful self-examination results in growth — his realization of his own responsibility. He comes to recognize this responsibility, both for the accident and, in a larger sense, for his own feelings, which had caused him to act as he did.

Uncertainty and, in particular, self-doubt, universal adolescent feelings during that period of great development, are continuously presented as the basis for Gene's internal debate. However, it is exactly these feelings that result in his learning so much about himself. This self-knowledge is the highest development, emotionally, of all. Through pain and a friend's death, Gene has come to know himself and his feelings better. Structurally, the reader is made aware that this process of growth and development has continued after the events in Gene's life at Devon, due to his return many years later, to examine his old school, and to think once again about the events that took place there.

Question 2.
In what ways is the war made "real" in the novel?

Answer
The war exists, physically, on a different continent than the school at Devon. Its distance is dramatized by Finny's refusal to believe in it at all, despite the constant talk of enlistment.

However, in small ways, its effects are felt at Devon — the absence of laborers, the clearing of the tracks for a train filled with troops, the teachers' patriotic speeches and, most graphically, in the newspaper and newsreel pictures that the students are constantly exposed to. These circumstantial details, together, make of the war an ongoing drama which cannot be forgotten or escaped, even at Devon.

The many sports, which play a large part in the daily lives of the boys, are "wars" in miniature, in which victory is, as Finny states, the essential thing. His invented game, "blitzball," becomes a dramatic illustration of the spirit of war — "since we're all enemies, we can and we will turn on each other all the time." That is, everything is changeable, and there are no unbreakable loyalties. This is again illustrated in the "Winter Olympics" snowball fight, another "war" in miniature.

Conflict is everywhere at Devon for the characters. There are constant challenges to everyone's courage, the primary one being the ritual jump from the tree. Leper is the only student who makes the actual "jump" into the army and, he, like Finny, becomes a casualty.

The trial scene in the Old Building resembles, dramatically, a war trial and, it, too, ends in a death, though indirectly. Finny's own agitation is the direct cause, but his upset is proof of a conflict within, which resulted from the war of opinion at the trial. Leper undergoes an actual trial by combat and, as mentioned above, returns in a very bad psychological state. His mental breakdown and his physical presence back at the school makes an actual connection between the school and the real war.

Lastly, the main character, Gene, is undergoing a perpetual war within himself, a conflict in which the enemy is hard to identify and defeat. This conflict ends in a form of resolution which is both painful and, at the same time, healing. Though it is an extremely hard lesson which Gene has learned, it is, in its own way, a peace treaty resulting from a victory within himself.

Question 3.
Discuss the similarity of the two "casualties," Leper and Finny.

Answer
Though relatively unconnected within the social framework of the Devon school, Leper's and Finny's deaths in the course of the novel force the reader to consider them as similar in some ways.

Outwardly, their characters seem very different — Leper is shy and a social outcast, while Finny is outgoing and aggressive, co-founder of the "Suicide Club." Of course, it is easy to suspect that someone so outgoing must be covering up some hidden insecurity, but the similarities between Leper and Finny are, finally, more in the fate they share than in their character traits.

Finny is "wounded" by the first fall, and Leper is wounded emotionally by the criticism and rejection of the rest of the Devon students. Each character suffers a second time — Finny falls again and dies as a result, while Leper experiences a profound breakdown due to his experiences in the war in Europe, and returns emotionally shattered. The first injury, in each of their cases, is received primarily as a result of the actions of others. The second and much more final wounding, for both Finny and Leper, is a result of their own actions — Finny flees from the "trial" and falls, and Leper decides to enlist. This is not, of course, to place the blame for their fate only on themselves, because each of their decisions was made in response to a social situation that they were involved in and reacting to.

Gene is the friend of both Finny and Leper and he experiences (first-hand) the suffering of each of them — physical (Finny) and mental (Leper). For Gene (and for the other students), Finny's death is a confirmation of mortality, as Leper's breakdown is a proof that there is a war out there in the world and that it is horrible and very real.

Neither Finny nor Leper, prior to his enlistment, consider the war as real. Finny directly and repeatedly states that "there is no war," and Leper is so distant from the reality of war that he goes hunting beaver dams instead of helping to clear the track for the troop train. Leper actually believed that if he enlisted, he would spend most of his time skiing in the woods. Finny denies the existence of the war right up until his death, and Leper's desertion is a form of denial as well.

In order to test themselves, both boys undertook actions which involved a certain amount of danger. Finny falls (with help, of course) from the tree, and Leper is "broken" by the war. Both students help, in the end, to bring the reality of the war and of the larger world to the school at Devon — Leper by his presence, lurking in the bushes and, Finny, by his absence.

Question 4.
Discuss the meaning of the "accidental" fall from the tree.

Answer
It is clear to the reader that the accident in which Finny falls from the tree is a symbol. In the narrative itself, of course, Finny's fall is just that — a fall from the tree. In those terms, it is a simple and effective way of moving the plot forward. However, the word "fall," suggests many levels of interpretation. Finny is a good athlete and popular at Devon. In a sense, he is "sitting on top of the world." The fall is thus a destruction of Finny's previous position, which will result in a reversal of his role, from sports participant to observer, and from an inventor of games to an inventor of new denials of the war. He must begin to build a shell that will protect him in his newer and much more vulnerable state. Thus, Finny, in his fall, can be considered a classic tragic hero, whose whole world has been turned

upside down. One of the functions of the tragic hero, in classical drama, was to provide an example for others, of someone who tempted fate. Finny provides an example for the other students of the reality of death and mortality and, thus, he is proof that the war did indeed exist.

The fact that the accidental fall is the result of Gene's shaking the branch, tends to imply that people, even friends, can cause a tragic situation to occur, and that the consequences can be much more than expected. Once he has fallen, Finny changes and can never be the same person again. This is proof to his schoolmates, particularly to Gene, that there are certain things which are irreversible.

The accident also brings up the question of responsibility. If Gene had not shaken the branch, then Finny might not have fallen. But it must be remembered that it was Finny who had originated the ceremony of jumping from the tree, and it was also Finny who insisted on doing it so often. It is the constant repetition of the ritual which had made Gene so frustrated on the evening of the accident, and it was Gene's frustration and resentment which prompted his impulsive gesture in shaking the tree. Thus, the accident introduces the extremely complicated nature of responsibility. Without the tragic fall from the tree, Finny would not have died the way he did. But, if Finny had not fallen from the tree, Gene never would have been faced with the necessity to examine his conscience and his feelings and learn from them as he did. Thus, the fall results in both good (Gene's development) and evil (Finny's death).

Question 5.

In the novel, there is great emphasis on a search for one's personal identity. Discuss.

Answer

The question of who and what one really is pervades the entire novel. Most of the characters change their ideas about themselves at least once. Leper begins with a lack of involvement with the war, and ends by a frightening flight from it. Brinker, the politician among the students, becomes more and more hostile as the book goes on. Finny struggles continuously to define himself as what he wants to be, but this involves not admitting certain things to himself. The reader is witness to

Gene's constant quest to understand more about his personal identity.

The war forces the students to think about what and who they are even more than they normally would at this time in their lives. It throws the external definition of each of the students (what others think they are), into conflict with each one's own feelings about who he is and what he is like. Each of the main characters has to prove his bravery by the jump from the tree. The background of the war and the probability of enlistment threatens each student, and causes each one to examine what he thinks of himself, to see if he is fit to fight in the war. Brinker becomes more and more fierce and argumentative, while at the same time, he begins to explain more often that he is only waiting for the right time to enlist. This is the result of his particular inner conflict.

Finny's idea of his identity is shattered when, after his accident, he can no longer be an athlete. He tries to force Gene to assume that identity for him but, Gene is, of course, undergoing the most strenuous identity crisis of all. His opinion of himself is shattered, too, by his role in Finny's accident. His feeling of guilt drives him to a painful examination of what he is and how he could have done such a thing to his best friend. He also wavers between thinking of himself as an athlete and as a scholar. The trial scenes force him to reconsider his role in the accident several times and he moves, toward the end of the novel, to a realization of the importance of the individual's judgment of himself. The judgment of others becomes secondary. Therefore, it becomes clear that, through a very painful and emotional process, Gene has moved furthest in his quest of discovery concerning his personal identity.

Question 6.
In what way is Finny a unique character in the novel?

Answer
Finny is recognized as unique early in the novel by his friend, Gene. He is a true eccentric, both in his actions and his attitudes. Finny, alone among the students, seems to have created a workable alternative to the war, and thus had avoided the unpleasantness experienced by all the other students to some degree, when they have to face the war. Finny never does.

He has the strongest, most original and inventive personality of all of the students — he is the inventor of "blitzball," and the originator of the "Suicide Club." This steadfast personality remains unchanged to the very end, and becomes a measure by which the reader can assess the changes in other students, like Gene, Brinker and Leper.

The strength of Finny's character is shown in his ability to both deny the existence of the war and to deny any responsibility on Gene's part for his accident. The world has tried, through school and personal pressures, to change him like the other students, and yet he successfully resisted all such pressures He was, in many ways, the most alive of all the students and the most able to enjoy life in its mixture of good and bad. Thus, his death presents both the other characters in the novel and the reader with an illustration of life's irony.

Finny, of all the students, suffers the least from any crisis of personal identity. He knows who he is and what his goal is — to succeed in his chosen field of athletics. The fact that he is first crippled and then dies, is a direct invasion of the horror and the injustice of the world into the lives of all the students at Devon. Finny feels the least mental pain and is the happiest of all the students, particularly in contrast to Gene and, yet, ironically, ends by feeling the most physical pain of them all. However, the inability of the world to cripple Finny's spirit becomes an important sign to Gene, who concludes that, in one way, Finny will always be alive. To Gene, Finny represents something essential to the spirit of living.

Bibliography

Crabbe, John K. "On The Playing Fields of Devon," *English Journal,* Vol. LII, 1963, pg. 109-111.

Ellis, James. *"A Separate Peace*: The Fall From Innocence," *English Journal,* Vol. LIII, 1964, pg. 313-318.

Foster, Milton P. "Levels of Meaning in *A Separate Peace,"* *English Record,* Vol. 18, no. 4, 1968, pg. 34-40.

Fuller, Edmund. "Review," *New York Times Book Review,* February 7, 1960, pg. 35.

Halio, Jay L. "John Knowles's Short Novels," *Studies in Short Fiction*, Vol. 1, 1964, pg. 107-112.

Hicks, Granville. "Review," *Saturday Review*, Vol. 43, March 5, 1960, pg. 15.

McDonald, James L. "The Novels of John Knowles," *Arizona Quarterly*, Vol. 23, 1967, pg. 335-342.

McDonald, Walter R. "Heroes Never Learn: Irony in *A Separate Peace,"* *Iowa English Bulletin,* Vol. 22, no. 3, 1972, pg. 33-36.

Mellard, James. "Counterpoint and Double Vision in *A Separate Peace,"* *Studies in Short Fiction,* Vol. 4, 1967, pg. 127-134.

Mengeling, Marvin E. *"A Separate Peace*: Meaning and Myth," *English Journal,* Vol. 58, 1969, pg. 1323-1329.

Nora, Sister M. "A Comparison of Actual and Symbolic Landscape in *A Separate Peace,"* *Discourse,* Vol. 11, 1968, pg. 356-362.

Raven, Simon. "Review," *The Spectator,* May 1, 1959, pg. 630.

Rosenfield, Claire. "The Shadow Within: The Conscious and Unconscious Use of the Double," *Daedalus: Journal of the American Academy of Arts and Sciences,* Vol. 92, no. 2 (Spring), 1963, pg. 326-344.

Ward, Hayden. "The Arnoldian Situation in *A Separate Peace,"* *The Bulletin of the West Virginia Association of College English Teachers,* Vol. 1, no. 1, 1974, pg. 2-10.

Weber, Ronald. "Narrative Method in *A Separate Peace,"* *Studies in Short Fiction,* Vol. 3, 1965, pg. 63-72.

Witherington, Paul. *"A Separate Peace:* A Study in Structural Ambiguity," *English Journal,* Vol. LIV, 1965, pg. 795-800.

Wolfe, Peter. "The Impact of Knowles's *A Separate Peace,"* *University Review,* Vol. 36, 1970, pg. 189-198.

NOTES

NOTES

NOTES

NOTES

NOTES

Don't forget to match that tough textbook with helpful
COLES NOTES
Expertly written, fast review summaries designed to give a greater understanding of the subject.

Shakespeare
Antony and Cleopatra
Antony and Cleopatra—Ques. and Ans.
As You Like It
Coriolanus
Hamlet
Hamlet in Everyday English
Hamlet—Ques. and Ans.
Julius Caesar
Julius Caesar in Everyday English
Julius Caesar—Ques. and Ans.
King Henry IV—Part 1
King Henry IV—Part 1
 —Ques. and Ans.
King Henry V
King Lear
King Lear in Everyday English
King Lear—Ques. and Ans.
Macbeth
Macbeth in Everyday English
Macbeth—Ques. and Ans.
Measure for Measure
Merchant of Venice
Merchant of Venice in Everyday English
Merchant of Venice—Ques. and Ans.
Midsummer Night's Dream
Midsummer Night's Dream in
 Everyday English
Midsummer Night's Dream—
 Ques. and Ans.
Much Ado About Nothing
Othello
Othello—Ques. and Ans.
Richard II
Richard III
Romeo and Juliet
Romeo and Juliet in Everyday English
Romeo and Juliet—Ques. and Ans.
Taming of the Shrew
Tempest
Twelfth Night
Winter's Tale

Shakespeare Total Study Editions
Hamlet
Julius Caesar
King Henry IV—Part 1
King Lear
Macbeth
Measure for Measure
Merchant of Venice
Othello
Romeo and Juliet

Taming of the Shrew
Tempest
Twelfth Night

Reference
Dictionary of Literary Terms
Effective Term Papers and Reports
English Grammar Simplified
Handbook of English Grammar
 and Composition
How to Write Good Essays
 and Critical Reviews
Secrets of Studying English

The Canterbury Tales
Canterbury Tales
Prologue to the Canterbury Tales T.S.E.
Prologue to the Canterbury Tales

French
French Grammar—Ques. and Ans.
French Grammar Simplified
French Verbs Fully Conjugated
French Verbs Simplified

German
German Grammar—Ques. and Ans.
German Grammar Simplified

History
History of Canada
History of the United States

Mathematics
Elementary Algebra Notes
Secondary Sch. Maths 1
Secondary Sch. Maths 4
Senior Algebra Notes

Chemistry
Elementary Chemistry Notes—Revised
How to Solve Chemistry Problems
Introduction to Chemistry
Senior Chemistry Notes—Revised

Physics
Elementary Physics Notes
How to Solve Physics Problems
Senior Physics Notes

Biology
Biology Notes

Philosophy
Philosophy—Ques. and Ans.

Literature/Poetry
Adventures of Huckleberry Finn
Adventures of Tom Sawyer
All Quiet on the Western Front
Animal Farm
Bleak House
Brave New World/
 Brave New World Revisited
Catch 22
Catcher in the Rye, Nine Stories
Chrysalids, Day of the Triffids
Crime and Punishment
Crucible
Cry the Beloved Country
Death of a Salesman
Diviners
Doctor Faustus
Duddy Kravitz and Other Works
Edible Woman
Emma
Fahrenheit 451
Far From the Madding Crowd
Farewell to Arms
Fifth Business
For Whom the Bell Tolls
Frost's Poetry Notes
Glass Menagerie
Grapes of Wrath
Great Expectations
Great Gatsby
Gulliver's Travels
Hard Times
Heart of Darkness
Ibsen's Works
Iliad
Jane Eyre
Joseph Andrews
Keats' Poetry Notes
King Oedipus, Oedipus at Colonus,
 Antigone
Le Morte D'Arthur
Lord of the Flies
Lord of the Rings, Hobbit
Madame Bovary
Man for All Seasons
Mansfield Park
Mayor of Casterbridge
Mill on the Floss
Mrs. Dalloway, To the Lighthouse
Murder in the Cathedral
 & Selected Poems